British Industry —

My Part in its Downfall

H. Rupert Feverdew

Published by Feverdew Press 2009
Copyright © 2009 Feverdew Press
www.feverdewpress.com

First Edition

cover image © 2009 Sharon Seymour
www. seymourart.com

Contents

Dedication

To my dear father who knew all this, after a career on the battlefield and in the War Office, who was good to his men and got the job done – after all we won the war, didn't we?

*****

Avec ses quatre dromadaires
Don Pedro d'Alfaroubiera
Courut le monde et l'admira.
Il fit ce que je voudrais faire
Si j'avais quatre dromadaires.

Guillaume Apollinaire, Alcools

Introduction

This is not a manual of how to do it, or even of how not to do it. It is simply a book to enjoy, and maybe to dabble in.

Everything in this book is TRUE - except the names, places, times, companies and products.

No malice is intended. So, if you recognise yourself - just keep quiet!

What went wrong

School days

When I was at school in the late 1950s we were taught by fine, dedicated staff who had been brought up in a world that no longer existed even then. They themselves had been brought up by parents who in turn had been taught by those to whom the battle of Waterloo was as distant a memory as the Second World War is to many today. The British Empire was still alive, in their minds, and the more recent memory of rationing, of mass production, of women working for the war effort, had not alerted them to the simple fact that they were marking time, soon to be gone, along with the era in which they still believed.

In Chemistry lessons I was taught about the Bessemer converter - a wonderful device for making steel, that foundation of our industrial revolution about which I knew and understood nothing. Only many years later did I discover that the Bessemer converter had a vogue of only about 20 years and was itself soon supplanted. Now, of course we have no steel industry at all.

Glimpses of industry

The biscuit factory that we visited from school, Huntley and Palmer, is no more. Do we still make biscuits, or are they flown in from India? the Far East?

We also visited two dark, satanic mills. One was Ford's factory at Dagenham, an appalling experience. The huge factory had no apparent order. Mired in filth, carcinogenic cutting oils and deafening noise it offered an unappealing prospect.

So did the Ever Ready battery factory we visited, where there seemed to be a hierarchy of horror and despair. There was no top floor board room with roof garden. Instead, as we went up through the building the working conditions got worse and worse. It seemed that the product progressed in the reverse direction, downwards, all the while getting cleaner until on the ground floor it was clean and neat enough to be sold. At the very top, on the fifth floor, the raw materials started their descent by a process initiated by black men shovelling carbon dust into a huge hopper. This dust filled the air, every surface and crevice. The men were in black dust on black clothes on black on black. They must have felt hardly human underneath. I felt ashamed.

As for us, we were a new and privileged generation - the first and maybe some of the last of those to get a really first-class education from the State. We had ambition, ability and optimism - a certainty that the world was waiting to give us jobs. It all depended on our own efforts. But those glimpses into British industry showed us that it was not so. There were stagnation, poor quality, restrictive practices and inefficiency on a grand scale. There was also exploitation of the poor, the unskilled, women and immigrants. The examples I had seen appeared to me to be single instances, unique experiences, but of course I was wrong - they were everywhere.

Choosing a career

Unfortunately there were definitely areas in which I would have liked and been able to make a contribution - provided that the economics and direction were right. These include the National Health Service - a visit to a general hospital (X-ray machines that appeared to have been made by Roentgen himself) put paid to that - and Education - a visit to a State Secondary School (typically three GCE passes per year for the whole school) put an end to that too. A lingering desire to do good and to follow the pull of one's own nascent sense of vocation remained, but only inside.

Modernisation...

In the 1980's, I attended a shipping exhibition, Europort, in the Netherlands. It made me cringe to see a government sponsored "British Ports" stand promoting some eighteen run-down establishments scattered round our coast which seemed hardly able to manufacture a rowing-boat. Opposite this stand were numerous Japanese stands demonstrating that ships could be designed and built by computer - each piece hoisted into position ready for welding, with apertures for the next beams and plates to be slid into place with millimetre accuracy, swiftly and cheaply. In my bones I had a sad, certain and correct feeling that this was an unrecoverable position for UK industry.

About the same time, the manager of a plant in which I worked decided to reform the production department and make it into a single, bright open plan expanse. This acceptance of a modern but much resented idea resulted in the demolition of a warren of jerry-built partitioned areas where management had evidently never before penetrated - one cubby-hole in the centre of the floor even had a bed in it. There was an area aptly named the Impregnation Room where, amongst other activities, young ladies applied varnish to coils of electrical wire.

...and stagnation

Meanwhile, not far away, at Southampton docks, people were being paid to play cards and drink tea all day long while colleagues in other trades went on strike, supposedly to preserve their impossible, obsolete way of life. They had not yet realised, and probably never did, that the invention of the shipping container and the aeroplane would have an irresistible power over their future.

At that time many large companies were still working on cost-plus contracts for various ministries, a method of payment which allowed overheads to be invented and inflated, and projects to be extended almost ad infinitum. One such example, the so-called "heavy torpedo" project went on for decades. Admittedly it did have a serious and perplexing flaw - it would turn round and attack the vessel that sent it!

Towards today

Nowadays, a similar ethos still applies in some areas — for example the government sponsored IT projects funded by taxation, supported by political patronage and cloaked in bureaucratic secrecy and dodgy deals.

The results are generally so appalling (CSA, agricultural subsidies, vaccination, patient records, ID cards and passports to name but a few) that it seems astounding that the public does not rise up against it.

But even the more obvious funding disasters - The Dome, the Olympic Games - seem to pass by or continue relentlessly with hardly a murmur. Perhaps we are just too used to these things - after British Leyland, De Lorean, Rover and the rest.

Though we now have more pressing concerns, the age of industrial strife is still not yet over.

My first and only direct brush with a picket line was as late as the mid-nineties. I was working as a consultant in a large industrial concern when one morning the works went on strike. An emergency management meeting was called for that afternoon. During the morning before the meeting, as a neutral non-staff member, I was able to wander down and mingle with the pickets outside the factory gate.

I was accepted by them as an objective and willing listener who, in addition, had the benefit of the ear of the management. I learnt the workers' point of view, which was based upon simple feelings of injustice.

Meanwhile, and at the start of the meeting, the management expressed among themselves a common feeling of disgust at the intransigent and unrealistic attitude of the workers.

I was astounded by the ignorance and confrontational attitudes of both sides. My explanation to the management meeting of the works views at first surprised them, but then attitudes quickly softened. A new approach led to a swift and sensible agreement.

Regrets

One cannot live life without regrets (as I was wisely told by one of my primary school teachers when I expressed my sorrow at not keeping up with another teacher whom I greatly respected). By the way, this wonderful unmarried lady had devoted her life to us children after losing her two brothers and her fiancé during the First World War.

For myself, I sometimes feel that if I had been stronger and cleverer I should have been able to make a larger personal contribution than I did, even maybe to have changed the course of British industry. On the other hand, there were plenty of smart people in positions of great power and influence that could and should have got it right, and stopped the decay, but none of them did.

Amateurism seems to me to be the one word which characterises much of the activity during the period from the 1960s into the 21st century.

Amateurism is in fact a fine and sometimes worthy British tradition. The ingenuity that was put into our war-time efforts in the Second World War - achieving victory with almost nothing - was barely short of miraculous. But our resources were utterly exhausted, and this approach could not build the peace. The post -WW1 efforts were not an example to follow. The period leading well into the 50s was a time of stagnation. Perhaps we had not been enough humiliated, unlike the Germans, to realise that we had to make a completely new and fresh start. Somehow victory was followed by a retreat. (Astonishingly, the wartime moneys borrowed from the United States had all to be paid back. This was only completed in about 2007.)

Then we had the sixties with their white-hot technological revolution. Innovation was everywhere, but many technical advances were triumphs of ingenuity over design, not a planned exploitation of science, nor of marketing. Almost every innovation was designed from first principles and didn't work very well. Lack of investment in production engineering and marketing meant that many good ideas were stillborn. A couple of generations later other countries have made the successors of many novel products into highly effective commodities with designs refined to superb reliability and mass-produced at a fraction of the price.

Our place in the world

Over the last ten years we have continued making new and quite unnecessary mistakes in the UK - reducing our expenditure on scientific education, research and development, and sending our capital plant to China to get the high technology commodities made over there, under the delusion that we will therefore get our product designs manufactured at lower cost and thus increase our profit margins.

We have thereby mortgaged our future. The Chinese have already learnt that they do not need our input to drive the process of technological advance. They can do it all themselves. Globalisation of the markets helps this process.

I am far from pessimistic but I can't help feeling that what is happening is a form of economic warfare - they are fighting us with our own weapon - capitalism. And as one wise person pointed out to me about the Chinese "they are very clever, they work very hard, and there are lots of them".

To the above one might now add "and they're sober". This is not a casual remark. It is a sad fact that the very large majority of our today's crime is fuelled by alcohol and drug abuse, leading to domestic violence and despair, with the danger of this being repeated into the next generation.

I've watched with dismay how the recreational drug culture here has taken over among children, students, and even university staff. The idea of applying chemical poisons to one's own brain was, if it was ever seriously considered, regarded as sheer folly by all of the enthusiastic and serious-minded students with whom I studied - totally contrary, by the way, to the common stereotype of student behaviour in the 1960's.

Nowadays one sees only too often the muddled and ineffective minds that result from an excess of pot smoking, and my own family has suffered the loss of young relatives and friends to the curse of hard drugs.

So, to amateurism one must add the failure of ambition, and the failure to look far enough into our the individual and collective future; an inability to recognise the need for change, determination and hard work.

Prosperity

At University I was taught that fossil fuels would run out at the end of the 20th century. We have had a few years of respite as new oil and gas discoveries have been made, allowing a huge increase in wealth in the West which was for some time able to control the flow of oil in our direction. The Middle East was happy to sell oil in return for "modernisation". Now the oil and gas reserves are truly reaching their end.

Even today our politicians are talking about a "mild and short recession" to be followed by "growth". It has somehow not been fully realised that the greatness of the West is almost wholly due not to skill but to the wholesale exploitation of natural resources. Alarmingly, this is understood by many in the Middle East who despise and hate our profligacy, and whom we misunderstand. Maybe the message of modest consumption and sustainability and its implications for the future remains too dangerous for our politicians yet to utter. It still seems electorally and politically too sensitive to contemplate telling people that they must become worse off.

However, we cannot continue on that path. We must consume less before we really do waste our planet, and maybe recent events will inexorably make that happen.

I am not sure that our politicians realise this. I do hope that some are more astute than they seem, but I doubt it.

The future

After the recent collapse of confidence in the financial systems of the USA and UK and the global repercussions, we can see that the social effects may be more immediate than many imagined. The credit crunch, toxic debt crisis, recession or crash, deflation or whatever it may be renamed in the near future, will selectively target the weakest amongst us and challenge the social structures aimed at providing a civilised level of mutual support.

In a recent newspaper report a scientist proclaims that the human race has finished evolving. I don't think so. Like in all living species subject to Darwinian laws change happens quickly when the environment undergoes rapid change. The rule is "adapt or die". On behalf of all living things, let us take up the challenge that the present offers and use our unique intelligence, not to try and change the environment, but to help each other to adapt to its inevitable change.

My optimistic view is that circumstances will soon force us to travel and transport goods much less. At the same time our new communication systems, still developing apace, may allow us to be personally fulfilled without such a need for physical movement across the planet.

We may also learn again how to use the earth to provide food for us close to home.

If so necessity and our ingenuity will in due course ensure success, though in a world we, like our forbears, might find it difficult to recognise.

Education

We all get it. Today we seem to get more of it but lower quality.

A few years ago it was decided that modern languages would be optional at GCSE. Last year the government became concerned at the decline in the take-up of language courses and is proposing an initiative to make it "more interesting" by lowering the standards, and starting pupils on languages at an earlier age. Now 30% less pupils study languages.

The decline in science teaching is even more marked. One third of all University physics departments have been closed during the last five years, while eighty percent of maths teachers have no maths degree.

Now, instead, we have social engineering. Pupils are to be selected on the basis of whether their parents have NOT been to university. This is despite the fact that university entrance has moved from being something for the elite 5% of A level grades to something to which 50% of young people can now aspire.

Standards have as a consequence fallen substantially. One can rightly argue that Universities are now doing a different and more widely "useful" job, with more emphasis on vocational courses and general education rather than research-based objectives.

But the currency has also been devalued by lowering the standard of A levels so that 30% can achieve A grades.

If you accept the argument (now being challenged from within the educational establishment) that standards have not fallen, then one must be forced to the conclusion that the exams are out of date. Today there is so much more that students need to know than thirty years ago. Through television and the internet young people can become better informed about the world and, at least until puberty, are keen to take part, learn and achieve.

I'm sure we underestimate our young people. They need to be set higher standards. Exams need to be graded both to provide evidence of achievement and to select the most able and stretch the imagination of the best pupils.

The idea of equality of opportunity is fine in theory, but people are not equal. School league tables offer no proper grading of added value and, by branding good schools with collective failure, often serve to demoralise teachers, parents and students alike, as well as creating the social divisions they seek to eliminate.

False assumptions include the idea that a school may be fairly judged on its results rather than its intake, and include a politically motivated failure to accept that children from rich homes may have inherited ability which may inherently sometimes lead to greater success.

In addition, grading students at any particular age misses out on the truth that children mature at different ages. A snapshot of performance takes no account of this or problems that an able child may have in their home life or relationships. Such tests are inaccurate both for this reason and because the tests are narrow and often have little value compared to a teacher's understanding of each student's stage and rate of development.

Rather than depriving some people of university places at an early age through testing or social discrimination, we should follow two principles.

Firstly to strive to compensate disadvantaged students for lack of adequate guidance and reading support at home, and secondly to allow the best pupils to achieve by firing their imagination and stretching them - something the National Curriculum singularly fails to do (also now recognised by a Cambridge University report).

The GCSE science curriculum has been watered down to make it "relevant". But while it contains material of general interest and value to the non-scientifically minded, which (conveniently) can be taught by non-scientists, it is not a good formula for developing scientists of the future.

My own view is that the idea of motivating pupils by making the subject "interesting" is a misdirection. Much more to the point, though more difficult, is to make young people realise that work is hard and they must learn how to do it, and that work is its own reward, and essential to their future.

The word work comes, by the way, from the old north country word "wark" meaning "to ache".

Unfortunately secondary school can be extremely boring. School is not a reflection of real life. Students must often find it difficult to see how the education they receive is going to serve them in the future. I think this is a major source of classroom indiscipline, frustration and antisocial behaviour outside, rather than the lack of sanctions such as physical punishment.

The governor

Sometimes teachers have an uphill battle. Here is a sadly modern approach to the classroom.

A classroom assistant sent a note to a parent complaining of her daughter's behaviour in class. The following day the mother was waiting at the classroom door.

Parent: "If you criticise my Charlene again I'll pull your ears off. And report you to the governors."

Classroom Assistant: "I am a governor"

A cheap lesson

I was five years old, the product of a second marriage of old-fashioned parents of great principle who had been born in the last years of the 19th century.

My parents had very high standards, including a manner of speaking which singled me out as a toff from the rest of the pupils at our rural village school. I used to walk the three miles cross country each way to school daily, on my own, though I always had a few pence in my pocket in case I wished to take the bus.

The journey to school took me through a wooded lane, down a hill, past a village shop where they sold petrol and paraffin from hand-cranked pumps, over a level crossing manned by a one-legged veteran of WW II who used to descend laboriously from his signal box to open the gates, sometimes only to hear a series of dings as soon as he descended which meant he had to return up the stairs leaving cars waiting even longer at the gates. (This crossing was the first in the country to become automatic.)

For those on foot like me there was a small side gate through which we could pass even when the cars could not, until it was locked remotely at the last minute before a train came by. From the level crossing the route took me up the side of a small sandpit and over a heath where one day I was bitten by an adder. At the end of the school day I would retrace my steps, sometimes lingering on the village green where there was a dewpond surrounded by tall rushes.

It was here that I learnt an important lesson. A boy from school approached me and told me that if I threw a penny into the pond he would give me tuppence. Being a simple, decent well bred boy I naturally took it for granted that he would do as he said and I tossed my penny into the pond. As far as I know it is still there.

Though I did not profit from this experience materially, it was an extremely cheap and valuable lesson.

Ambition

Ambition is necessary, but like science and religion, it can be used for good or evil.

Everyone has an aptitude, a talent. The most fortunate people are those whose interests and aptitudes coincide. They have a vocation. If this is discovered and encouraged at a young age then the motivation and ambition they feel can almost certainly ensure that they have a fulfilling and happy future in their chosen subject.

For some less moral and often less able people, ambition is achieved through the exploitation and domination of others. They are grown-up versions of the school bully - indeed they are one and the same - insecure, inadequate, dishonest - and through the early discovery that their methods intimidate and neutralise the capabilities and influence of others – they are both arrogant and dangerous.

Without the least cynicism I can say that I can't find anything humorous about this kind of person. The only saving grace is that they often move on soon from your corporation, though never soon enough, and, sadly, usually before being found out. They thus continue to do damage elsewhere - usually on my patch. How this happens contains another important lesson.

In order to avoid it happening it is essential to take personal references in the right way and from the right people. That means people other than those the candidate puts forward themselves. The past employer but one, by means of the telephone, is a good start.

Ideally this checking requires some independent investigation. It is worth $200 a day (or much more) to get a James Rockford onto the case. What you will find out won't take too long and, were you to be in the TV business, could make you a couple of interesting episodes!

Unfortunately, in the real world, the problem has often got its origins long before - because each job acts as a passport to the next one. "If he's done that … then he must be good".

The operation and survival of the Peter Principle is assured by this kind of thinking, so beware.

Smoking

I worked for nearly five years for a highly talented, technocratic, ambitious north-country man. His ambition was to get onto the company's parent board, but it was obvious that his technical skills and training were inappropriate and irrelevant to that higher level of financial management or manipulation.

He worked incredibly hard to achieve his aim. Before very long he had a serious heart attack, at the age of thirty six, and another fatal one shortly after. Stress was a major factor, but I now realise that the more important and direct cause was heavy smoking.

The stress and ambition inherent in his personality were of course the underlying reasons for his demise. I recall that he never once used the words "thank you" to me. I was paid to do what I did – the pay packet was the reward, and contained the only thank you required.

Like mother, like daughter

A daughter at prep school went to the adjacent junior department to see her mother who, after a sparkling career, had become a mum and held a part-time post as a class-room assistant there.

Daughter: "Mum, we had a talk on careers today"

Mum: "Good, was there anything you fancied?"

Daughter: "Yes, I said I wanted to be like you"

Mum: "That's nice, but what specifically?"

Daughter: "I want to have lunch and play tennis"

Motivation

The fear motive is rightly derided today as an old-fashioned repressive method from the days of the sweat-shop. I believe that the most important personal qualities in an employer towards their employees (or a parent towards their children), in addition to determination, are consistency and fairness. Every employee needs to know where they stand, to understand the likely effect of their actions and to know how his or her decisions and actions will be perceived. This is especially true if the mission is demanding and the stakes are high.

The fear motive does however have its place as a means of control.

The black spot

The proud mother of a girl at preparatory school went to see the maths teacher, who had applied a black spot to the child's homework, and assailed him with the following comment:

> "What do you think you are doing? She's worked her f***ing ass off - and it's Racist!"

It may be relevant to add that the girl in question was very small and blonde and went on to ballet school and a successful career in dancing. Maybe her mother's determination had something to do with her success - but not as a mathematician.

Recruitment

Most employers adopt the principles that I shall describe, though they may not recognise them formally. The interview remains the most common and most misused and imprecise form of personnel selection.

An employer seeks three things from a prospective employee – qualifications, experience and the right attitude.

If your candidate has all three then you need to be aware that they do not really want the job. They may feel they need it right now because of adverse circumstances, but that is only a temporary need. They will soon want to be somewhere else.

Let's look at these three qualities in turn.

Qualifications are important. They are evidence of success in following a course of study, of dedication and perseverance. They are suggestive of a possible professional approach, but they do not ensure that the candidate can do the job. For the interviewer selecting a candidate who demonstrates the right qualifications, relying on qualifications provides a reasonably safe option, and a weak but sometimes plausible defence when things go wrong - provided of course that the qualifications are genuine, which cannot be relied on even at a senior level.

Experience is also important. A candidate who has done a similar job, or part of it, may have a better approach than a raw recruit with wonderful qualifications. A candidate who has lower qualifications but has learnt on the job is likely to understand the world of work. If they have qualified through part-time study they will be able to demonstrate ambition, dedication, stamina and the ability to work hard in difficult circumstances.

The right attitude is not only important but essential. You and your employee must be able to rub along well together. The employee must be able to take the initiative, feed back essential information and check with you before taking major risks.

They must be able to communicate the results of their work. They must avoid the tendency to squirrel away knowledge in order to become indispensable – such people are never indispensable but they can be a damnable nuisance.

They must be able to get on with colleagues and show charm and professionalism towards your customers and suppliers, to accept their own position in the organisation and be supportive of you.

They must be able to make people want to do things for them and show good personal judgement.

In short, they should in due time be able to do your job and to provide you with success and understanding of all the essential elements of their responsibilities to ensure that your own performance is rated highly enough to ensure your promotion.

So, if the ideal candidate with all three qualifications does not exist and you cannot do without the right attitude, which do you go for – qualifications or experience?

This is your task, and there is no general solution. You will have to work out the solution for yourself.

For the candidate, a little understanding of the threads of thought that will be going through the mind of the employer will prove invaluable. As a candidate it is your task to make the prospective employer feel good about you; to assure them that you are both a good worker and a safe pair of hands.

The advertisement - your own job

The company accounts were two months late, again - it was a fiasco. The accountant was suffering from stress. He came to my office to show me an advertisement for a tempting local job. I agreed with him that the time had come for a change and suggested that he apply. What I failed to tell him was that, though I had no prior knowledge, it was perfectly obvious to me that it was his own job that was advertised. I nipped up to forewarn the Managing Director.

The CV - revealing yourself

A CV should avoid platitudes. When I see the words "I like working with people" in a CV, I jib.

The employer needs to know not what your title was, but what you have done, how well you did it, whether you enjoyed it, and what you want to do in the future. If you have researched the post and say in your CV what is relevant to the prospective employer and to the job brief you will get an interview. Fatuous generalisations lead nowhere except to the waste bin.

One candidate put down "beer and sex" as his hobbies. (I'm sure he was being honest.)

A foreign candidate wrote at the end of his supporting letter "and good luck to you too", a charming sentiment with perhaps a hint of cultural differences to be overcome.

The interview - the wrong job offer

On the temple of the oracle at Delphi is written the good advice "Know Yourself". This wise dictum is the key to planning, to controlling, and thus to predicting your own future. Clear self-knowledge gives you a higher level of free-will. But how hard it is to be objective about oneself.

Asking the right questions of the prospective employer early in an interview will enable a mutual understanding to be developed - after all, the interview is a two way process, not an examination. But if I hear that statement "I like working with people" I will reply "Oh, really? I hate people!". This always provokes a revealing, disbelieving reaction and demands an explanation. This explanation can break the ice and start a real dialogue.

If there is something inappropriate in the CV (maybe I didn't read it right) or the candidate's responses suggest that they are not right for the job, I will discuss this with them so as to save wasting everyone's time. It also helps the candidate to realise that their rejection is not necessarily a failure on their part, and it may also help them be more realistic or clearer in their CV in future.

The wrong job - again

Upon leaving University various interviews were set up for me. One was in a granite pile on the Thames near the Strand, the London office of Unilever. I was offered the job of Brand Manager for a soap powder at Port Sunlight. It was hinted that this could be the first rung on the ladder to the boardroom. The salary and training would be excellent.

Would I have made a good Brand Manager? Would I have enjoyed the job, the place? Did they really need me? I doubted all these and sent a polite letter of refusal. Shortly afterwards I received a pleasant letter wishing me good fortune in the alternative offer that I had taken up. There was no such offer.

Preparation is everything, not only for interviews but for all kinds of encounter. For even the most quick-witted it is difficult to control an encounter without preparation, and this can be serious if it is an important meeting - often there is no opportunity for correction or explanation.

If I have an awkward situation to deal with or a difficult telephone call to make, I will prepare a check-list and ensure that all the points are covered during the conversation, marking them off as I go. I can thus control the conversation and am able to progress my argument logically and efficiently. Thereby I can ensure that what the other person says does not divert me from my plan, and can deal immediately with any opposition.

Interviews are often not well planned or well-structured by the prospective employer, so you can make a good impression by having your own thoughts organised. Also, while it is difficult to research a company in advance, you can collect plenty of useful information at the interview by preparing your questions.

One performs best at interview if one is indifferent to the outcome, or at least can maintain a high level of objectivity. Desperation can be detected instantly. It is also important to keep one's antennae waving - to pick up positive and negative clues.

the wrong job again ...

At a second interview for a new job I was taken by the Sales Director to see the plant of which I was to become manager. He was so evasive, on the grounds that so much was hush-hush, that I was little wiser after the tour. I wrote a letter complaining to the Managing Director.

I received a friendly and reassuring response from the MD, together with the job offer. What I had not picked up was that the two of them were Freemasons, and were together manipulating me to plug a serious hole in the organisation which they had so far found extremely difficult to do.

... and again ...

At one interview I was put into an empty ground floor room to fill in a questionnaire. I was appalled by the ludicrous questions. One was "Write down a list of possible uses for an empty shoe polish tin". Others were more intrusive, in the style of "When did you stop beating your wife?".

I started to imagine how I would open the sash window, trip carefully but quickly through the rose garden below, lower my head while passing the reception office window and dash for my car.

Unfortunately I then recalled that I had left my coat hanging in reception so that a more traditional and polite exit was required.

... and again!

During a second interview at another company I went with the HR Manager and two other managers to a pub for a ploughman's lunch. When a stranger entered the pub, leaving the door ajar, one of the managers got up, gave the door an almighty kick and shouted "Can't you shut the bloody door!!!".

This dangerous and uncouth man, to whom I was later to report until he suddenly got the sack and disappeared without saying goodbye, had huge influence through his position as a Director. His offensive manner and bizarre suggestions were able to destroy the decision-making process of any meeting that he attended.

Later, quite by chance, I came across him in his next, new job - running a corner shop on the Northampton ring road.

Establishing rapport

Establishing rapport between interviewer and interviewee is very important. The interview is a highly formative point in the future relationship, and is never forgotten. If you cannot establish a common understanding early on the relationship between you is unlikely to flower.

A loan

To save a prospective employee losing time and money by travelling some twenty miles for an interview I suggested meeting at a local pub close to where we both lived. Arriving at the appointed time I found him already sitting there, very smart and a little nervous. After friendly introductions I asked him what he would like to drink and went to the bar to order, only to find that I had brought no money. The candidate offered me a loan - he had to, really! It was a good ice-breaker, and he got the job. Occasionally, when he wanted something I was reminded of this incident, though never in anger.

Who are you?

I was sent for an interview by an agency, with the location and company name, but was not given the name of the person who would interview me.

I was ushered into a plain office by a secretary and introduced to my interviewer by name. Still not knowing his position in the company I asked him and was told that he was Chairman and Chief Executive. My friendly and relaxed reply "Oh, that seems like a good place to start" was well received.

I was offered a job one level up from that for which I had been put forward. I later learned that almost everyone in the organisation was terrified of this good man, a highly moral Methodist whom I greatly admired.

The Mad portfolio

Taking a portfolio to an interview, except in obvious special cases such as artistic posts, is in my opinion counter-productive. Too often documents or articles offered are irrelevant, out-of-date, tired and tatty, or, to an experienced eye, unconvincing. Describing what you did is usually much more effective, and has the great benefit that it can be changed on the fly to suit the questioning.

One candidate for an engineering job brought with him his MSc dissertation on an electronics topic. When I opened it I was surprised to see a copy of MAD magazine fall out onto the desk. On the cover was that cartoon image of the bizarre face that is so often adapted to caricature President George W Bush.

During questioning it turned out that this candidate was the road manager of a well-known pop band.

The seriousness of his application was in some doubt, and, fairly or not, I felt an unacceptable risk. It was a "No".

Albert and the Lion

I was interviewing a very smart young man of African origin for a post as an Electronics Engineer. He was seeking a post for an industrial year during a degree course at a good provincial University.

To get the conversation going I asked, using a polite question tag "This would be your first job in electronics, wouldn't it?".

The candidate answered "Yes, that's so, but my last job was very exacting". "Oh," I responded curiously "In what way?". Well, I was working on a game reserve in Tanzania, and two of my colleagues got eaten". He got the job.

It later transpired that one colleague had been trampled to death by an elephant. An angry elephant can run very fast and no escape is possible, even up a tree. They just push it over.

The other colleague had fallen prey to a practice that had become common among the wardens at a visitor centre on the edge of the reserve where the tourists came wishing to photograph the lions in action.

For the lions there it was an easy life. Lazy by nature, they would lie about in the shade expecting to be fed from time to time, avoiding the bother of hunting.

In order to rouse the lions from their apparent stupor the guides would offer for $50 to go and kick one of the lions and run swiftly back to their four-by-four which was parked 25 yards away with the driver's door open.

On this fateful day the lion was not asleep, knew what to expect and was not in a good mood.

Not wishing to wait to be kicked up the backside it launched itself at the guide and, according to Albert's account, hit him so hard with its huge paws on his fleeing shoulders that the blow had broken his neck, so that he was probably dead before he hit the ground.

References

Nowadays it is inadvisable to put anything negative into a written reference - so what's the point of them?

Faint praise

Quote from one referee (possibly apocryphal) - "You will be fortunate indeed to get Mr Smith to work for you".

Subtle – not!

From a French reference - "Il y a des lacunes dans son ignorance"

The contract of employment

Never give a sales rep a new car. The purpose of this rule is simple - to quell the sin of pride.

The dented reputation

A newly appointed sales rep was given a new car and took a secretary out at lunch-time in it. Parked under a tree they got into a clinch. Unknown to them a small boy was in the tree.

In order to spy better on the couple he moved out along a branch, whereupon the branch broke and he and the branch fell onto the car, denting the roof.

Vanishing contracts

Working without a contract is a very bad idea.

A letter of appointment is the minimum essential requirement. It forms an important temporary contract, but even so needs to be carefully checked.

But you said ...

A youngster I know worked for a week for a company that paid her £2 an hour less than she was promised verbally at the start of the week.

Are you still here?

When an assignment of mine came to an end I worked out three months notice. Near the end of the time the boss suggested a new project and asked me to prepare a draft contract for myself and a project proposal, which I duly did and submitted. No response was received.

I continued carefully to research and detail the project proposal, based upon the wish list from the boss. After a little extra research I came to the conclusion that the original idea was flawed and that the project could not succeed.

I sent a memo to him to this effect, with an argument explaining my conclusions. Still no response...

My original leaving date at the end of the month passed without comment, and with no contract. I pondered what to do and continued with my other departmental duties, as I had a responsibility to a team of engineers who had been told nothing of this situation and my possible departure.

After some ten days I enquired again about the proposed project and was told that he agreed with me - the project was impractical. It was to be abandoned. I would not be needed, and would I please take another three (tax-free) months pay in lieu.

Moving expenses - Carpets

A good way to blight your career is to do a smart deal with your new employer. A colleague did this by taking the company up on an offer to pay for carpets for his new house. He had the whole house carpeted with top quality wool for a sum that exceeded his annual salary. In fact he did not last the year - the boss remembered it with venom every time he looked at him.

The boss's wife

I fell into the same trap as the man with the carpets.

Actually, I thought my problems were because I had failed to recognise the new boss's wife at a party, which is bad enough, but my wife reminds me that it happened much earlier.

The new boss had refused to pay my relocation expenses when the company moved, and when I made representations to the Group HR Director my boss was over-ruled. I got my expenses but was never forgiven.

Apprenticeship

By apprenticeship I mean "apprentissage", the process of growing up, maturing. A first job can be an ideal place to do this.

Value for money

My first job was one summer in a Standards Testing Laboratory at a time of expanding technology, research and of Product Standardisation. The magazine and organisation "Which?" had yet to be born.

I was paid £5 a week to test lamps from cars, lavatory seats, bloodstained motor-cycle helmets and other assorted paraphernalia of modern life. The jobs used to come through in job bags containing documentation which included the value of the job.

By means of a personal "time-and motion" study I was able to carry out the optical tests on the car reflectors and lamps in a way of my own invention rather than that I had been shown (a laborious process which involved turning lights off, waiting until one's eyes accommodated before taking a reading, and again before writing down the result and inserting the next sample). By preparing everything it its right place at the outset I could do the whole job in the dark, by the tiny light of the photometer, without moving from my workbench.

In the first day I had completed £200 worth of work. Soon I had done all the tasks that it was foreseen that I would be capable of. A key moment.

The boss, an amiable but distant, perhaps haughty, man was a true British eccentric. He always wore a bow tie. He had large paunch on which a monocle hung from a ribbon round his neck dangling or lying, according to whether he was touring the works or leaning back at the luncheon table. It would be heartless to say he had some batty ideas. He was very successful.

Mushrooms

The laboratories had a huge tensile and compression testing machine, an Olsen - a lumbering giant suitable for the foyer of the Science Museum. The boss wanted to understand how mushrooms could break their way through cracks in tarmac - had they some mysterious strength? I doubted it. (It is the host tree roots that break through.) But I was constrained for fear of the sack into performing a series of experiments on some fungi from the car park. Did they withstand a huge force, even a small force perhaps? No, they just flattened, leaving a few fibres and a slight ooze on the machine. There was to be no paper in the Mycological Journal.

The next task had to be done after dark. Could one spot the pollen of bracket fungi in the light of a torch? As it was summer-time the evenings were light. Success required a long wait into the evening and finally a pleasant tramp through the woods. Bracket fungi were found and tapped while the torch was played on the underside. Nothing… (The pollen are microscopic.)

But these activities did not fully occupy my days or nights. I was regarded as a willing collaborator, a true scientist and promising engineer.

Bees

Between my other tasks I was requested to mend the boss's bee-hives. They had some loose panels which required to be nailed down. No smoke or headgear was offered.

Only Winnie-the-Pooh hanging from a balloon had a more dangerous task. An attempt at emulating Pooh's nonchalant approach was necessary. I went forward giving the appearance of fearlessness. I did not get stung, but a number of bees got their stings stuck into my woolly jumper so that I, being naturally kind to living things, sat for some time near the hive to give them an opportunity to unwind themselves.

This was the end of my career as a pioneering mycologist, apiarist and upholder of Standards.

Why you were hired

If you apply for any senior post in another organisation, I will assure you that your prospective company has undoubtedly got a serious problem.

What is their problem? At interview they'll tell you some of the "whats" but rather less of the "whys". The latter you will have to work out for yourself.

What are the possibilities? It could be that the present incumbent has fouled up big time, or they and the boss have just had a quarrel, or panicked, or the boss is out of his depth, or simply that they THINK they can't solve it by promoting someone in-house.

Whichever way, you may have a major problem coming up. This is especially true if the problem is the missed internal promotion, as the boss has already created enemies for you in the camp.

The glass partition

On starting an assignment I was given an office next to my predecessor who was working out his notice after a disagreement with the Managing Director. We were separated by a glass partition.

For the first day he sent me e-mails on company matters, with just a hint of bitterness in them.

On the second day I replied to one of his e-mails saying "I think we ought to talk, don't you?" This response enabled us to team up and exchange useful information about the reality of the company's situation and gave me an opportunity to sooth his battered ego.

Even if the employer's objectives are worthy - for example there may be a genuine need to recruit because the company is expanding - you have to be prepared to realise that your understanding of and perspective on your role will soon vary from the original brief.

After three years it is likely that you will be bored, complacent and ineffective. You've solved the original problem and the company is moving in a direction that no longer presents a challenge to you or matches your skills and needs.

If the company is not large enough to make a change of role possible for you, you both need a change.

I believe that a company should look hard at its structure at least annually, like a spring clean, to avoid stagnation and stop a slow accumulation of problems becoming a crisis.

The first day

The first day is like every other day, except more sharply in focus. It can also be the last.

A quick job

At a research laboratory a new laboratory assistant was being shown round the building by a shabby, balding man in a dirty off-white lab coat. The laboratory was a modern award-winning building with covered cloisters round a pretty well-tended central garden with a fish pond - an ideal arrangement for taking someone on a circular tour.

Unknown to the new recruit, his guide was a very senior member of staff. It was certainly not a good idea to tell anyone that though he had applied and been accepted for a permanent job he didn't want to stay. He would be leaving to go to college in the autumn and only wanted the job for the summer. The tour was completed. The guide said to the new recruit

"As you can see, we're back at the front entrance. Please go through it and don't come back. You're fired!".

The whole process had taken under ten minutes.

It can take even less than that.

No job at all

The Managing Director had taken on a senior manager. The letter of appointment had been sent. One morning the elderly owner of the company woke up with a change of mind. Without discussion with the Managing Director he came in to the office early and got one of the secretaries to write a letter telling the manager not to come. I don't know whether the unfortunate appointee had resigned his job, or sold his house …

The three-legged mongrel

Starting in a new job, if you are successful in getting that far, can be very daunting. You feel that everyone is an old hand whereas you don't know the ropes, and that everyone is sizing you up and likely to make a hasty, adverse and long-lasting judgement on you before you have time to find out where to hang your coat.

A more serious worry is that if you actually do something, especially in a first job, you will not be confident that the result will be what you intended. You have to make those first, perhaps far-reaching decisions (or that is how they feel) with an almost total lack of understanding of the facts of the business or the good character and dependability of those around you. You dare not ask your boss what to do in case he concludes you are an idiot. Here is a solution that was kindly presented to my wife when starting a job in a country solicitor's office.

The client, a well-to-do lady, had a pedigree dog which had been savaged by a three-legged mongrel owned by a working man. Both the mongrel and its owner were definitely of a lower class to the lady and her injured dog.

The task of my wife was to satisfy the client by preparing a threatening letter to the owner of the mongrel, claiming that he and his mongrel were wholly responsible for the injury and should compensate her for vet's bills, anxiety and miscellaneous consequential expenses, or else be sued and hung up by his thumbs for a month, and so on…

A draft letter was duly prepared and shown to the boss. He approved the proposed letter, which was itself very persuasive, and then offered a further suggestion.

A second letter should be written, to the lady, attaching a copy of the first letter and advising her that everything possible had been done but that realistically she had no hope whatsoever of obtaining compensation.

Working for a large corporation

In the desert world of the meerkat, social structure and hierarchy are very important. These structures have been developed to enable their groups to operate and interact effectively without the ability to communicate through speech.

Sharing human understanding, even with verbal communication, is often just as difficult. The verbal messages may differ considerably both from the body language and from the underlying thinking.

Our society has its essential formal social structures. Terrible things can happen when these break down - for example in Russia, Iraq, Zimbabwe, in a company or in an orchestra. It is therefore important to understand the dynamics of your group - in this case the company in which you are employed - most of which will be unstated and based upon assumptions, some shared and some hidden.

In the meerkat world there is a dominant male who has sole mating rights. The other males have to content themselves with a lower rank and generally forlorn hopes in that direction, except by subtle deceit. A female who strays from the group and mates with an outsider will be banished. She must survive alone. The roving male that has abandoned his group appears to take pity on her. He will groom her and stay the night in the burrow, but in the morning he has gone roving again.

You have been employed to do a certain job within your group, and you will need to think that you understand the value and purpose of your task and to go home feeling that you have done it well. And it pays to know the rules.

However, at the very top of the company things are different. The plant in which you work is an enclosed entity whose existence is governed by the laws of the market. The rules for success are simple - monitor and control the finances tightly and employ specialists to run the operations. If market conditions are understood and exploited effectively then all will be well.

Unfortunately this is not the complete picture. If things don't go as planned the plant is likely to be closed, suddenly, regardless of any consideration for you or your colleagues.

Also, there is a secret agenda — namely the self-interest of those that control the company. This may be completely at variance with what you think is the common aim for which you are honestly toiling.

Fixing the share price

The directors are close to retirement and want to increase the share price. A series of dubious acquisitions, with the benefit of good PR, causes the share price to double. However, it is discovered that one foreign acquisition, purchased for £12M in today's money, had been bankrupt at the point of purchase. The company taken over had used the purchase money to clear its creditors on the very day of purchase. This had been cleverly concealed by a supposed postal delay in transferring the papers to the purchaser.

The truth took a little while to emerge. Claimed purchase orders of over £4M did not exist (though the purchaser's production department started building the products). The orders were entirely imaginary. Also, real estate that the purchasers thought they were acquiring had been split in two. Half had been secretly retained by the sellers, together with the most valuable plant and stock assets. The company had bought a pig in a poke.

The auditors, a leading City name, were at fault for not carrying out due diligence correctly. However, because of the appalling errors and misjudgments and the inevitable embarrassment and potential fall in share price if disclosure was made, not a word was said and the directors retired in peace. You can imagine what happened to the company shortly afterwards.

The overnight move

In the 1980's it was reported that a factory had been relocated over one weekend without any prior notice to its employees. The directors' idea was that if anyone got wind of the operation there would be an unpleasant outcry amongst the workers.

There was no follow-up story in the newspapers, so I can't tell you whether it worked, but it can't have been easy for those left behind.

The alternative, giving six month's notice, as happened at a place where I worked, was also highly damaging. It became a matter of honour to get another job, and more and more difficult for the remainder to continue as key staff dispersed. Only one fifth of the staff stayed through the relocation, though to be fair, that is what the directors wisely or unwisely wanted.

A tiny blip

The plant manager and accountant may overvalue the stock to tide them over a brief cash flow blip (such as a late order) but if the problem persists (the order is cancelled) then it becomes more serious.

A former accountant of a company at which I worked slashing his wrists when this practice could no longer be concealed. It seems hardly worth it to me, though I understand that his mental state was disturbed by some complicated woman trouble...

Training

Training is probably the most important thing that a company can do for you, and for themselves.

Get as much of it as you can. It can offer you new perspectives, skills and confidence. Above all, training is transformative. It is the key to the adaptability which is more than ever needed in the modern world.

The trouble is - these benefits can be life-changing. The cost of training is therefore often resented by the employer. It is an overhead which is easily cut if other areas overspend, and having training gives the employee greater bargaining power in the job market. Your company instinctively recognises and either consciously or unconsciously wishes to suppress it.

Sponsored training

A promising Sales Manager had undertaken and completed an Open University degree in his spare time and at his own cost over a number of years. No recognition was given in salary or advancement for this achievement.

On completion of the degree the manager asked the employer to support an MBA. A deal was struck. One condition was that the fees would be repaid to the company if the employee left within a certain period.

During the following year the manager worked large amounts of unpaid overtime and spent many months overseas away from family with neither bonus nor holidays and he decided to leave. Prolonged and stressful negotiation finally led to a waiver of the fee.

An important part of a manager's training is to learn to give clear instructions. You should not make any concessions as to what you think your employees might or ought to know.

Nor should you make assumptions about the employee's ability to perform the task required, nor fail to check that the job has been done as requested.

Such assumptions are only possible once you know your employee well, and even then need to be modified according to the importance of the job.

Posting an urgent letter of value or importance is a case in point. If it must go out first class within the next half-hour, it should, in my opinion, be taken to the post only by you in person.

In summary - you can delegate a task but not the responsibility.

Hamish's wheelbarrow

Hamish's wheelbarrow, the title of the following anecdote, has become a family expression. Its application is now ingrained in our methods of working.

I worked as a weekend volunteer at a Rare Breeds farm, a charity supporting and accommodating disabled people. As I was mucking out a Shire horse I was approached by one of the residents, Hamish no less, a simple, friendly and enthusiastic young man, and asked if I had any jobs I would like him to do.

"Yes" I replied, searching around for a suitable task, "You could take this barrow of manure round to the tip".

Ten minutes passed, during which time I was unable to continue as I had placed my shovel on the barrow for his use, and I contented myself with amusing some young visitors.

Finally I realised my error - he would never come back!

I had failed to give him a complete and adequate instruction, namely "Please go to the tip with this barrow, empty it onto the pile and bring back both the barrow and the shovel immediately after you have done that."

Commuting and working away from home

Though not strictly part of the job, commuting is something on which most of us waste a lot of productive energy, time and money.

It is good if you can live close to your work, and these days this is a major consideration. The uncertainties of life nowadays mean that moving for the job is usually unwise. It may even be impossible if it is not funded by your company. So ideally the job should move to you.

Many of us could work from home. The main reason that this doesn't happen more widely is lack of trust - your company won't trust you to work, and, even if they do, someone will think or subtly suggest that you're shirking and take advantage of your absence. You will be uncomfortable about this. And you will miss those all-important meetings and the snippets of intelligence gleaned at the coffee machine.

I'm not sure that there is a complete solution to the problems of working from home. The technology is there but building trust is difficult and takes time, or maybe for ever. The only sure solution is to work near to home. This permits different approaches to commuting.

The smell of horses

I've known people come to work by horse, but the steamy smell of warm tack is very unpopular in the Ladies Room. A colleague used to come in by canoe, carrying it the last few yards on his head.

Under the bench

I've also heard of someone sleeping inside a bench in a chemical laboratory while arranging lodgings. Another acquaintance used to sleep in the office at his first job in the music industry, simply because he enjoyed it so much and was fearful of losing his position. Some years later he's still there - in the job, that is - but now he's the boss.

Shane

Lodgings can be fun – they are much more interesting than hotels. At one such establishment I used to take the landlady's Alsatian, Shane, for a walk every evening. Shane was a good companion. I taught him to say woof to get me to open the gate on our return.

One evening I was walking ahead of him when he shot past me with a loud yelp. Turning round, I could see no obvious reason for this - the road was deserted.

On retracing our steps I discovered tell-tale evidence on the metal cover at the base of a concrete lamp-post. When marking his territory he had shorted out the mains supply to the lamp. The landlady, a sensitive soul, was not as amused as I when this was recounted.

Suitcases at dusk

Contracting can be a mixed blessing. The pay is good, but the hours are long. The travelling can be very arduous. One day you have work; the next you have none. When a job comes along you've got to take it. This can be hard if you have other unfinished projects. This was the case when I got a weekly commuting contract at the other end of the country...

I got up at six o'clock at home on a summer Sunday morning and went straight along the landing to my office to continue with the completion of an outstanding project. My deadline to leave for the airport for my new assignment was 6pm, allowing for 7pm check-in, 8pm departure, 9pm arrival, 10pm in the hotel and so to bed. At 5.40pm I packed a suitcase, snatched a hasty supper prepared by my wife and set off on time at 6pm.

In the airport departure lounge I was interested to notice that a well-dressed lady passenger had a soft bag identical to that in which I was carrying my laptop computer. (I had selected it so that it did not look like a computer bag, and thus would not attract muggers when in city side-streets. It could also, if necessary, be used to "handbag" a mugger.)

On arriving at the destination airport I collected my main suitcase, similar in style to my hand baggage, from the carrousel, and made for the Underground with the two bags on a trolley.

While going down the ramp to the platform I suddenly had a feeling that the stitching on the larger case looked slightly different from my recollection, and I stopped to open it. Sure enough it wasn't mine. It was filled with alien and disturbing objects - ladies paraphernalia, dresses, lingerie and suchlike. I dashed back up to the now deserted luggage collection area, and noticed a lady, indeed the same lady of the aforementioned hand luggage, looking rather concerned at the counter of the information kiosk.

Together we soon established that the case I had was hers. And there was mine, lying alone on the floor near the carousel.

My concern was not, however, over. What a coincidence to have two pairs of identical bags, she warbled!

Yes, she was going on the Underground. Let me carefully put them all on a trolley and we'll go to the station together.

Yes, she's going on the same line, in the same direction.

Dispensing with the trolley we stood on the station platform and carefully separated the bags. But soon I started to feel even more uncomfortable - the lady was standing much too close, inside my personal space.

A train arrived and we both got on. The doors closed. She sat next to me, again too close. I started to wonder whether we were going to get off at the same station. I hoped not but said nothing. She, on the other hand, started saying "Wouldn't it have been funny if we hadn't found out about the cases? What would we have done?" Slight titter.

My discomfort increased a further level, but to my great relief she got off at a station before me.

I thought that was the end of it and sat back in a taxi to my hotel where, as a regular visitor, I was greeted warmly. I ordered a prawn sandwich and a gin and tonic at the bar, stayed there a while and then went up to bed.

I opened my case. Yes, it was mine. I started to undress.

Suddenly I was startled to realise that I had obviously been giving off the wrong signals to my female fellow traveller. I was already, or rather still, in my striped pyjamas under a V necked jumper.

I had gone straight into the office in the morning in the pyjamas, and worked, head down, all day. My wife had brought me lunch and supper and seen me off hastily without noticing that anything was amiss.

The Fawlty tea house

It would require a John Cleese with a team of forty to choreograph this remarkable burlesque.

In the High Street of a Dorset town there is a B&B. Through a simple pillared portico in the warm brick façade, with a huge spiral ammonite over it, you enter a smart hallway.

To the left is the lounge. Further down, also on the left, is a spare room which at the time of this story was filled with furniture while the upstairs was undergoing a make-over.

Going straight on, the hall opens through a doorway into a large farmhouse kitchen beyond which is a pretty walled garden with a door in the mellow stone wall leading into a side alley.

Today's guests include, besides me, a couple of rather deaf, genteel old ladies who are taking afternoon tea in the lounge and watching the television, and two rather earthy engineers from a civil engineering contractor, arriving early from work and extremely drunk.

The engineers, who are in no condition to drive, have been sent back to their lodgings in a taxi. Outside the house is a lamp-post and for some inexplicable reason one of the engineers is clinging to it, refusing to go into the house.

A small team, including me and the landlord, is sent out into the street to detach him from the lamp-post and to get both of the engineers into the house without disturbing the ladies. Having prised the one off the lamp-post the two of them stumble along the hall. Then one falls through the doorway into the spare room, noisily scattering a pile of chairs within.

The landlord pokes his head round the door of the lounge. The subterfuge is successful, so far. The ladies are oblivious of the drama and have attributed the noise to the sound track of the black and white slapstick film showing on the television.

Meanwhile the other engineer has returned to pay the taxi and commissioned the driver to go and get two portions of fish and chips from down the road.

In the absence of the engineers a brief conference is held in the kitchen. The landlord decides that the engineers, now both paralytic, are not safe in the house and they are carried through the garden gate and out into the back alley to sober up.

Then there is a loud knock on the door.

The fish and chips have arrived and the taxi driver is paid off. Clearly the engineers are in no state to eat their food, so it is decided that it should be eaten by those still present. I am to have one portion and this is dispensed onto a plate. I rather anxiously start to eat it at the kitchen table.

Elsewhere the establishment is busy. Other guests are expected, but also it is feared that the engineers may regain consciousness and may be searching for their bed and board. Each time there is a knock on the door I grab my plate and slip it out of sight onto my lap under the table.

We get through supper without a hitch.

My hosts then kindly introduce me to the local Conservative Club across the road, for a good evening's drinking before daring to return. All is calm back at base.

Hunger pangs

Understanding cultural differences is an important part of foreign travel.

In Japan they eat rice. This will not surprise you. But in Japan they do not bake anything and that surprised me. So after 10 days of my visit I was getting extremely hungry. Rice does not provide enough stamina for a substantial Westerner. I therefore decided to have a beef steak in my hotel, despite the very high price.

It was a huge and superb steak, but very difficult to eat with chopsticks. I found a knife and fork and cut some small pieces off the steak, but I determined to get into the local mood and eat as much as possible with chopsticks.

I set to.

Under the steak were some interesting beans, shaped like broad beans but black, obviously a local speciality.

Gripping one of these beans between the chopsticks, with some difficulty, I popped it into my mouth and then quickly out again.

The "bean" was excruciatingly, blisteringly hot. It was a stone. The steak had been laid on hot stones to drain the fat.

Meetings

Meetings rarely achieve much. They are only necessary because people don't talk to each other in civilised and productive ways in informal settings. And people often seem to be unable to make decisions.

Part of the cause of this is that managers work mostly within their own departments.

I have always felt that a company should have a "management department" where daily, perhaps starting with morning coffee, the management decisions and actions of the company as a whole should be planned, reviewed and disseminated to the departments.

Instead, everyone goes straight to their own department on arrival, to further their own ends rather than the common good. As a result, problems can accumulate for a day or a week rather than being nipped in the bud.

If people did communicate properly a formal meeting should rarely take more than ten minutes and the record of the meeting, if any, would simply note the actions to be taken in the future.

Instead, life being by its very nature inefficient, the discourse drags on into attempts to make detailed plans, predict the unpredictable, design the product, resolve or create misunderstandings and ambiguities, to pose and to play-act and to jockey for position.

A good example of the useless meeting is the quarterly one at one establishment where I worked which was known as the "Oh Christ" meeting. It took place just before board meetings. Its sole purpose was to agree "what the hell shall we tell them this time?" A more effective (but potentially more dangerous) way would have been to have the "pre-meeting" after the board meeting to agree on future actions arising from board decisions, but this would not have had quite the same frisson.

In France, I understand, meetings are apt not to close formally with decisions. Instead people drift away as they lose interest. The decisions are made elsewhere over coffee or lunch. If this is so then there is much merit in it. For most of us, even the most highly intelligent, it is good to "sleep on" problems before making decisions.

A delay enables the wisdom of a decision to be considered, new facts to be collected and weighed and, in the French manner, debated further.

Many business actions agreed at meetings never happen, simply because those involved realise afterwards that the decision was wrong - it won't work. And another meeting is needed to put it right. It is meetings in general, or the chair of the meetings, that get the blame.

Like I said at the beginning, meetings rarely achieve much.

Conversely, many correct actions can be taken without a meeting. If all the necessary facts are available the correct decision is usually obvious.

The tape recorder

For those with little speed of mind, taking notes is a prop that does little good.

One engineer was over-promoted into a powerful but dangerous position as head of a major new division developing products of a highly technical nature (which finally led to the downfall of the parent company).

He used to put a small recorder onto the table at meetings. This even happened at a business dinner which I attended in a good London restaurant with him and the company chairman, the first time I met him.

At this meeting he recounted how difficult his sixteen year old son was. This young man was deficient in that he did not understand his father. Communication between them was problematical or non-existent.

I was not surprised. But, as must have happened at many meetings with (or without) the recorder, I said nothing and so he continued in ignorance of the impression he was making and the effect of his non-communication on his business.

The pocket memo

Another senior manager, who did not last long at his post, had a small stitched leather memo pad into which slips of paper could be slipped. It had a narrow pocket down the side to hold a pencil.

Whenever a discussion started he would take out this device from an inner jacket pocket and, instead of digesting the argument, he would make notes in a tiny crabbed hand as an aide-memoire.

I guess he thought that reviewing these would enable him to understand the ideas behind the words, but it never did.

The act of taking notes was itself the problem. He was too busy writing to listen or understand to what was being said.

Colleagues

This is a random walk through just a few examples of the many fascinating people and variations of the human condition that I've encountered.

The handyman

The delightful and courageous works handyman was becoming increasingly troubled by Parkinson's Disease. He was told by his doctor not to climb ladders, but did. He had great difficulty opening doors, on account of the intention tremor. However, he was not to be deterred. One of his brave techniques was to get on his bike at home, somehow, and pedal to work.

Because of the difficulty of getting off the bike in a tidy manner he would drive over the pavement onto the front lawn of the factory and tumble gently onto the grass.

The lovesick deaf-mute

The company employed a deaf-mute. He was a talented though under-educated young man. He could hear nothing and was unable to utter more than a few noises.

He had great skill and patience, and was the only person in the factory who could perform several highly delicate and essential tasks.

On this particular fateful day he came in with an anguished expression, beating his chest and making agonising noises. Assuming that he was seriously ill an ambulance was called. He was taken to hospital where his perfectly healthy appendix was removed.

His real problem was his heart. It was broken. But who was the object of his affections? I never knew.

The banker

One dashing young colleague, who enjoyed a sports car and an overdraft to match, was called in to see his bank manager who in a state of exasperation made the following statement to him "Mr Woodstock, the bank would much prefer it if you banked with us rather than we with you".

The surgeon

A young apprentice maker of surgical instruments decided to try one out on himself, by removing a large wart from his knee, at his workbench. He was half way through the operation, carried out without any anaesthetic or antiseptic precautions, when the MD passed by with an important foreign visitor. Our amateur surgeon had got to a point where he was forced to continue, much to the interest of the boss, visitor and colleagues.

The optimist

Another enthusiastic apprentice was asked by the MD, once again accompanied by a visitor, to explain what he was doing - something very impressive and technical. The enthusiastic apprentice replied not just with a factual account of the work but added an explanation of how excellently he was progressing and how speedily he could do it. He expected to finish it within fifteen minutes.

A week later a similar visit occurred. The apprentice was still working on the same item. He was ever after known by the name "15 minutes". This was not an insult, but a cautionary reminder. He was a delightful companion and became an excellent engineer.

Bell's Palsy

Things were very tough in the works. Business was brisk but deadlines were approaching. Extra time was being worked. Stress levels were increasing.

One employee contracted a mysterious ailment known as Bell's Palsy wherein one side of the face becomes paralysed. This particular victim had to put a sticking plaster over his eye at night to keep it shut.

The medical cause of this condition, which is fortunately temporary, is not known. However, the very excitable Spanish wife of this employee knew better. She telephoned me in hysterical but broken English to give me a lengthy harangue. It was all my fault - I was a cruel and uncaring slave driver. Her husband was a sensitive, precious person, not to be taken advantage of, not employed to take this kind of stress. Be warned, she would hold me personally responsible for any further mishaps that might befall him.

I was quite impressed, but I rather think that at home he himself was the target of similar invective.

The genius

Gentleness, lack of guile, generosity and abstraction from the day-to-day world characterised this charming and recognised academic genius who had, by accident as much as by success, fallen into a senior position in the bear-pit of British Industry.

When I got married he sent me from abroad a cheque for a substantial sum of money. He accompanied it with a short note addressing me by my surname, Feverdew - the first time he had ever addressed me in this old-fashioned and respectful academic usage. He was too shy to break into real intimacy.

He used to stand in the foyer of the company on his right leg, looking up at the ceiling, or beyond, wondering which way to travel next. His left hand was stretched behind him holding onto his right foot. He was perfectly balanced. Periodically he would let out a brief sound "Tyoup!", a sound which punctuated some new question, milestone or decision in his thinking. Suddenly he would release his foot, sweep a lock of glossy grey-black hair from his forehead and shoot off in his selected, or maybe a random, direction.

On one occasion that I recall, shortly after my own wedding, this direction was towards the reception kiosk.

There, the receptionist who was to be married the following weekend sat watching him as he took out his cheque book and Parker 51 fountain pen from an inner pocket. Half kneeling in front of her he made her out a cheque to the value of £10, some £50 at today's value. He then gazed upwards in his usual dreamy manner, and quite innocently crossed out £10 and substituted £5.

The Fresnel lens

In the early 1970s my boss was an affectionate, frugal and unselfconscious man with a charming wife. They used to spend their winters in the United States in order to avoid the worst of the British weather, and during a business trip over there I was invited to stay at their simple but beautiful New England wooden house. The firm, which they owned, was run prudently and without extravagance.

In those far-off days most televisions were very small, and theirs was no exception. It was a cold April; no groundhogs to be seen, but flurries of snow outside, and the electricity supply, being 117 volts and at the end of the distribution line, was providing little warmth from the electric bar fires.

In order to provide simple amusement the couple decided we would stay in for the evening and watch television.

My boss was an inventor, and, like me, an admirer of Thomas Edison. In order to make up for the deficiency in the size of the television which was placed on a chest of drawers near the foot of their bed he had invented a new means of television viewing. A Fresnel lens was suspended from the ceiling in front of the television.

For the benefit of the non-technical I should here explain that a Fresnel lens is a highly magnifying lens in which one surface has circular steps on it, rather like those huge ones that are used in front of the lantern in a lighthouse. This one was rather smaller, than that of a lighthouse, just a little bit bigger than the television screen in fact.

One of the disadvantages of a Fresnel lens is that it has a very narrow field of view — it is okay if you are looking straight in line into the middle of it, but, like an old-fashioned computer monitor, it is of little use if you are off-axis. (Another obvious disadvantage, which doesn't matter in a lighthouse but does in a television, is that the image is superposed with a series of blurred rings!)

These matters proved no deterrent. After a nourishing supper we three repaired to the master bedroom where we lay chastely side by side under the covers, with our heads as close together as possible, to view the television.

The Great Dane

A smart, aristocratic young gentleman, newly appointed as Sales Manager, decided to show off his status and personal superiority by bringing his Great Dane into the factory. (He proved not to be a roaring success at his job - one of his less good ideas was to give Green Shield stamps with the scientific instruments.)

He would walk haughtily up and down the production floor between the yellow lines early in the morning to review the troops before retiring to his comfortable office. (The machinists, I can report, were less than impressed by this.)

Unfortunately on this particular day the huge dog, which by this time was familiar with the layout of most of the works, decided to explore some new territories and pushed its way through the swing door into the ladies lavatory. Unable to get out, it got claustrophobic, then hysterical, barking and howling and throwing itself against the door. On the other side the ladies from the assembly line, with crossed legs, started to get equally frantic.

After this incident he was ordered not to bring the dog in again, but this was not before another notable event, described below.

The icy morning

One icy December day we had a visit from the Managing Director of the company's largest and most important customer.

The Sales Manager and he, plus the Great Dane, set off for luncheon at a local restaurant. The dog was standing in the middle of the back of the car, with one enormous paw on the back of each of the front seats, eyeing the road and slavering into the ear of the visitor.

As the car approached a roundabout it failed to respond to the brakes as intended, but instead slewed off the road into a ditch. The Sales Manager broke his arm, while the dog flew forward onto the visitor's lap and emptied its bowels there.

The caravanner

We had a factory supervisor with only one leg. It had never occurred to me that such a disability would interfere with conjugal relations until he told me over a cup of tea in the canteen about his Irish holiday in a gypsy caravan. The inside of this round-topped caravan was constructed with vertical hoops of ash onto which were connected horizontal slats to strengthen the structure.

While making love in happy holiday spirit to his dear wife he somehow got his good leg - well, the only one - stuck between two of the slats in such a way that neither of them could move to release it. How the matter was finally resolved I have forgotten, I regret to say, probably because I was crying tears of laughter.

The hitch-hiker

The son of the company's owner had, in a manner of speaking, grown up, and having acquired a substantial inheritance he bought a motor business which he renamed according to his unusual surname Van der Hulst Motors. On the walnut fascia of his sumptuous Jaguar car was affixed a small brass plaque announcing that it had been supplied by him at the said garage. Being of both a proud and kindly disposition he was apt to pick up hitch-hikers.

On one occasion a hitch-hiker noticed the plaque with interest and said "Oh, he was at the same college as me". "Oh, that's interesting" replied the driver, "tell me more". "Oh" says the hiker, "he was a complete plonker" and continued to relate a number of lurid examples of his foolish behaviour.

To his credit, this tale was told to me by the driver himself.

The architect

The attraction of employing someone you know and think you can trust can be tempting. Resist it - it is always a mistake. It is a bad sin, called nepotism. The reason it is so dangerous is that your friend is sure to foul up - everyone does from time to time.

But your friend will be mistrusted if the connection with you is known, as it always is. Because of this they are much less likely to be forgiven for errors. They have a mountain to climb. Their misdeeds will be exaggerated and laid at your door. Your reputation will suffer, and when you finally get rid of your friend from the firm, you will be likely to lose a colleague, a friend and your reputation.

The owner of a small company brought in an architect friend to apply some "industrial design" to some small and intricate technical products. The poor sap was totally out of his depth and soon derided by all and very soon went the way of all such misfits, though not before causing some consternation.

My abiding personal recollection, among the corporate disasters, is of his lisp. Passing by our house at lunchtime one day I invited him to share our meagre repast, some soup and a roll. "Would you like some more soup?" I asked. "Thooper" was the reply.

The squaddie

There is an army saying "Shoot first and ask questions afterwards". Training to control fear and react instantly to threats is a very useful skill.

There were three people working in the laboratory when a high pressure hose came adrift at one end and started thrashing about and hissing as gas spurted from the loose end.

By chance I was standing outside the doorway and witnessed what happened. One person ran away, a second stood rooted to the spot. The third, an ex-corporal, rushed forward, jumped on the hose and bent the end over to stop the leak.

All this happened in less than five seconds.

The hang-over

I used to take two colleagues to work in my company car. I was the line manager of one of them. On this particular day this one was in the back and was clearly unwell. He was groaning slightly and shading his eyes from the early morning sun. It was apparent that he had a severe alcoholic headache.

Our other companion said something about "the hair of the dog" to which I added the teasing and as it proved particularly unhelpful remark that I thought that gargling with a raw egg was an excellent remedy. At this point, before we could stop, the poor chap was violently sick into his lap.

The convict

I was working on a new catalogue for a client and was told by the boss, privately in his office, that I would soon be working with another particular employee. It was explained to me that this person had just come out of prison for something to do with pornography and grievous bodily harm. Upon enquiring why he had told me this, he replied "I thought it might be useful".

The placenta

Working in a medical company, I had just acquired an arrogant and useless new boss (nepotism again, I think). Somehow he sported a doctorate, a non-medical PhD. He was Dr Tapper and he was out to impress.

We were on a visit to a famous European teaching hospital to visit a leading professor. Unknown to Dr Tapper I had already met the professor and had established good working relations with him, planning a clinical trial.

As we were approaching the professor's office Dr Tapper drew me aside and said "Don't forget to introduce me as Doctor Tapper", to which I assented. Our introduction was only semi-formal - "Good morning, Alvin. Good to see you. Can I introduce Dr Tapper."

This strategy is not one I would recommend, but little harm was done as Dr Tapper soon engineered his own demise.

On the same occasion, shortly afterwards, we were going down a hospital corridor of the obstetrical unit, in which uncomfortable sounds of women in labour could be heard, when a door opened and a nurse came by with a placenta in a kidney-bowl.

Dr Tapper turned a greeny shade of grey.

Momentarily I was not sure whether to catch him or let him fall.

The vanishing book-keeper

A new book-keeper was brought in on contract to deal with a temporary vacancy. Shortly afterwards a permanent book-keeper had been recruited. The contract book-keeper, who had been hoping to make the post a permanent part-time appointment, was not proving a great success.

In fact he had entirely unknowingly brought the company to its knees. More than a month's worth of invoicing had been "posted" into the accounts but not into the mail before the omission was discovered. A major cash crisis followed, and the temporary book keeper had changed the password on the accounts system so that, amongst other things, no-one could be paid.

He was working part-time elsewhere and was difficult to get hold of. Also he had not yet been advised of the permanent appointment.

I was away from the office and left a message for him to telephone the necessary password confidentially to a lady named Doris.

Instead he decided to visit in person. On arrival he found to find the new book-keeper, Doris no less, sitting in "his" chair. I'm told that some kind of scene followed, but I never got another communication, nor an invoice, from the contractor.

The blind take-off and landing

I wish to pay tribute to a (real) great man, W E P "Johnny" Johnston. In his later life when I knew him he was a patent agent. Before and during the war he had been an effective contributor to the war effort, including involvement in the design of the undercarriage and other essential developments for the Spitfire fighter (anticipating the folding mechanism later used to influence the design of the first McLaren baby buggy).

He was also the first person to do a blind take-off and landing in an aeroplane, which he did in a Tiger Moth biplane with a blanket over the windscreen and instruments that he made and fitted himself. I attended his funeral at the Air Force church, St Clement Danes, in Fleet Street, where a soprano in the gallery movingly sang Bach's beautiful song "Bist Du Bei Mir".

Flying westwards

Flying his plane due west on Salisbury plane Johnny would over-fly the route of the railway line from Andover to Salisbury. The prevailing wind enabled him to fly very slowly over the trains, and he would fly so low over the engine of a steam train that the engine driver would throw lumps of coal at him. Eventually there was a complaint and he was forced to atone by sending a crate of wine to the Stationmaster at Salisbury.

Sympathy

A young engineer of some twenty-one years suffered from cystic fibrosis, for which he had periodically to spend some time in hospital to have his lungs cleared.

A card was bought and circulated round the works. When it arrived on my desk a number of signatures and messages had already been entered. In order to avoid duplication and get some ideas for a suitable contribution of my own, I scanned the messages. One particularly caught my eye and caused me to draw breath. It read "Die, you bastard".

Complacency and fatalism

For many years I thought that everyone was ambitious and that those who did menial jobs did so because of sheer necessity and a bad throw of the dice in life, rather than lack of motivation. But I was proved wrong.

For some twenty years there had been a daily works bus service between the main factory and a subsidiary plant about ten miles away. A draughtsman, who supplied designs to the main factory, told me that he had never been there and didn't want to.

But times were changing, hand draughting was giving way to computerisation, and even greater changes were afoot. Only a few of us, as we thought, knew that the plant was to be closed. The cleaner, who always kept himself well informed, came into the drawing office one day holding his broom and announced:

"Great news, chaps. They're closing us down for Christmas".

I wonder whether that draughtsman ever worked again after the closure. I'm sure the cleaner did.

The skull-cap

A new nuclear power station was being commissioned. It was months or years behind schedule and every day was adding many hundreds of thousands of pounds to the bill. An instrument had failed - our equipment was thought to be at fault. Its function was critical to shutting down the reactor rapidly in the event of a coolant leak. The instrument in question turned out to be one of the original "type test" instruments that had gone through intensive testing some eight years previously.

It was decided to do a test on a new sample instrument by connecting it to a long high-pressure steam line and suddenly opening a valve to see if it would be damaged by the pressure surge. In preparation, the representative of our customer, a Jewish gentleman, took a small skull-cap from his jacket and placed it on his head, for luck.

I had no such prop but the experiment was a success - there was a sudden violent shock but no damage occurred.

Further enquiries soon established that the cause of failure was that someone had forcibly over-ridden an interlock system aimed at preventing just such an eventuality.

I heard of another incident in the same plant where analysis of corrosion of a pipe showed that the cause was someone urinating on it. I was less surprised than some when I heard about the Chernobyl disaster.

A misunderstanding

Things in life are rarely black and white.

To be able to see the other person's point of view is a valuable quality. Sometimes, however, this is very hard, as people will rarely tell you what they are thinking. It may be best not to jump to conclusions, but to "keep one's powder dry" and see how things develop.

I was working on a project for a well-known importer of consumer goods. The collaboration of the Finance Director appeared essential to the success of the project, but he was reluctant and irritable. I thought hard about this. Should I complain to the Managing Director about the man's obstructiveness?

I decided on another course. After all, I thought, it is my job to find solutions for the MD, not to create problems. I chose to elicit the support of the very keen number two in the finance department and the project proceeded successfully.

Three months after completion, during a visit to carry out a review, I experienced a strong emotion on seeing the Finance Director again.

He was clearly very unwell. He was thin, gaunt, hollow-cheeked, pale. One word came immediately to my mind - "cancer".

I was so glad that I had taken the course that I had. Maybe the MD, or all of them, had known all along.

Secretaries

Secretaries are untouchable. You already know why, but here is a reminder for the tempted.

Secretaries know much more about the company than you do. They are no fools. Also you do not know with whom they are already sleeping. It could be the boss. Like I said, they are no fools.

Knowing who's who

When visiting a well-known client company by train, as a consultant, I requested a lift back to the station and was driven there by the receptionist. She informed me that the Production Director, whom I had mentally labelled as rather incompetent, was married to the Chairman's daughter. Important information!

If you want useful but sensitive information about a company it is generally better to ask someone other than a secretary.

For example, engineers are an excellent source of opinion about managers, sales, marketing, HR, production and the financial health of the company.

Salesmen, on the other hand, will tell you willingly about the competence or otherwise of the engineers, whom they sometimes regard almost as another species.

Appraisals

I have only had one appraisal in my life, and this was in a company in which I was not an employee but a consultant. Often the results of appraisals are signed and put away in a locked file and forgotten until the next year.

The spayed cat

The boss, the Managing Director, announced that it was time to do appraisals and as I was there wouldn't it be a good idea if I had one too.

I happily agreed to this intriguing prospect and the time duly arrived, for which an hour had been allotted.

About half way through the process of assessing my capabilities under various abstruse headings, the boss looked at his watch and announced:

"Sorry, I must go, I've got to take the cat to be spayed".

That was the end of the appraisal. I never heard any more about it.

Exhibitions and demonstrations

Everyone who has ever tried to demonstrate a product knows about what I call "exhibition-itis". To summarise - the damn thing seems to recognise the importance of the occasion and like a mule just decides that it won't work!

There are other hazards, too...

The blue dye

The Managing Director had somehow got involved in demonstrating a new product - itself a bad mistake for someone in his position. This demonstration involved a tall tube of water, about 4 metres high which had been coloured blue to give extra emphasis and clarity. Attempting to demonstrate the power of the device he turned the wrong tap and the blue liquid shot out of the top and poured all over his head, suit and white shirt.

The underpants

A major exhibition in a European capital city was attended by all the big international players, plus their suppliers and contractors and, further down the scale, the suppliers and subcontractors to the contractors. A representative of one of our suppliers was there, and, sensing a huge potential up the supply chain, volunteered to pay for the wine at our evening meal in a smart restaurant. Unfortunately he did not see the sting coming - the wine was £400 a bottle. But that was only the beginning...

One of my colleagues said that he had found two girls, and would I like to come out with him and meet them. We arrived at a very gaudy chrome and glass bar populated by over-painted and under-dressed girls, keen to make very awkward small talk and sell more outrageously priced drinks, and so on…

It was quite obvious that we had strayed into a very seedy and rather worryingly unpleasant side of this dynamic capital. Not used to such city lights I was too scared to go down to the toilet in the basement on my own and asked to be accompanied by my colleague. Nothing untoward occurred. After a while, it fortunately became clear that his girls would not turn up. We were able to leave pure, and unsullied, with our reputations and wallets relatively intact.

Our supplier was not so fortunate. I'm not sure where he went after the dinner. There was never an adequate explanation, but in the morning at breakfast he complained that he was without underpants. They had disappeared without trace during the night.

The actuator

The Managing Director went to the USA taking with him the prototype of a new type of actuator to demonstrate. The performance of a major product depended on this device which had been assembled just the day before - another serious error.

When it failed to work the following fax was received in the Sales office. "Design bloody awful!" it screamed. Of course the Engineering Director was the last person in the organisation to become aware of the arrival of this message and its dreadful import.

Unplugging the competitor

The company had had great difficulty in designing a particular coupling so that it could not be disconnected by the user while under pressure. Going round a trade exhibition I noticed one of our competitors prominently exhibiting a similar product. Assuming that they had successfully solved this rather tricky problem I was determined to get a good look at it.

Waiting discreetly nearby until the stand was crowded with visitors, presumably potential customers, I sidled onto the stand and unplugged the connector in question. There was a very loud bang and a rush of gas. They had not solved the problem! It was difficult to slip away unseen.

The smoking gun

In the 1970's, long before smoking was widely banned, on a trip to Japan with the chairman of our company we learnt various new skills such as squatting on the floor at meals without dislocating our hips.

Today we were positioned near our company's stand in the exhibition hall adjacent to our Tokyo hotel. The chairman, a gentle, affable pipe smoker, found a chair nearby in which to settle for a quiet smoke. No sooner had he struck up than a guard strode up, screaming, gesticulating and pointing a handgun.

It emerged, with difficulty, that the chairman was sitting in front of a painted hieroglyph on the wall, whose message was "No smoking".

Grappa

No-one will dispute that the Italians, on the whole, are a delightful, generous and welcoming people.

On a week's trip there I was plied from our agent's office cabinet with unaccustomed alcoholic beverages almost from the moment of my arrival. There was a warming pre-prandial at midday, at least half litre of good wine with the lunch, then a couple of potent grappas after lunch. This routine started again at teatime and went on through dinner and late into the evening.

The result was that I was semi-inebriated the whole week.

The equipment I was demonstrating worked fairly well until my hosts started to poke about and remove circuit boards from within its enclosure. When I took back and replaced one of the boards I did not realise (until I was back in England and cold sober) that I had re-inserted it incorrectly. In fact the board had no keyway to prevent incorrect insertion. The product never worked again during my trip, though I felt, perhaps unjustifiably in view of my condition, that I had talked my way successfully out of danger.

The golf trainer

I was not present at the event recounted here, but I know the protagonists and the incident has stuck indelibly in my mind.

An enterprising Sales Director, some time in the early 1970's, thought that he could make a mint for his company in the leisure industry by making and selling a golf trainer. The device he envisaged would comprise a circular platform to be placed on the ground, with a captive golf ball on a stalk at its centre and some dials which would indicate the direction and distance that the ball would have travelled had it not been held captive.

A prototype device was constructed. A launch venue was selected on the front lawn of a smart nearby country hotel. Local dignitaries, press and prospective customers were invited. It was a warm summer afternoon.

A little speech was given and then the Sales Director, a good golfer, strode forward to demonstrate the device. He took a great swing and hit the ball squarely.

The ball detached from the platform and disappeared into the trees, upon which the Sales Director shouted "Oh, fuck!", threw the remainder of the machine into the boot of his car, slammed it shut, and drove off leaving all the others behind in a cloud of dust and gravel.

Making the sale

The lettuce leaf

The salesman was in a new job. He had visited the representative of a promising prospect, a bright young lady who could make the purchase decision for her organisation at a provincial university town. Soon everything was agreed in principle. To oil the wheels he suggested that they go out to lunch. The deal would be signed in the afternoon.

Over lunch the conversation drifted away from work.

Salesman: "Oh, yes I know the University well. I was there between such and such."

"Oh yes, I was there then, too."

"I lived in that village"

"So did I" and so on… It was a small community.

"Whereabouts did you live in the village?"

"In the square"

"Which house?"

"My goodness, so did I"

By this time the salesman was starting to get very worried and starting to sweat. It was clear that they had lived in the same house, maybe at the same time. But he couldn't remember who she was.

But he could remember many embarrassing incidents of his student days. Maybe he had disgraced himself, made a pass at her, or worse...

Try as he might he couldn't remember, and half of him didn't want to. But he had a feeling that she knew more than she was letting on.

Things were getting out of control. The deal was rapidly flying out of the window.

The sweat on his forehead was becoming very obvious. It was time to wipe it off.

Looking nonchalantly elsewhere he picked up what he thought was his napkin and mopped his brow with it.

It was a lettuce leaf.

Telling the truth

To develop a long-term relationship between a customer and supplier requires trust and understanding. This means that you have to tell the truth. As in other walks of life the truth will out. It is always less painful to clear the air by holding up your hands and saying "mea culpa!".

I was working in a company trying to build a complex engineering system for a major utility. To the customer it was quite a small project, but to my company it represented a major opportunity and the livelihood of many people. Nothing seemed to be going right, but I was convinced that it could be completed and made to work.

I was careful to let the customer's Project Manager know exactly what my plans were and the state of progress. Only in this way could he take appropriate action and maintain his own position with conviction.

In fact he had a vested interest to champion the project, which was a significant innovation, if only it could be made a success. Not many months later when it was finally installed and working, he said to me "You know, Rupert, if it hadn't been for you we would have pulled the plug on the project long ago".

Office dinners and parties

Everyone has memories of office parties that would be best forgotten. Here are some of the more amusing that have slipped through my personal filter.

The ice bucket

The senior management were having a dinner at a local Chinese restaurant. One of the managers, a European thought to have good taste in matters gastronomic, was detailed to select the wine. When it arrived it was presented and accepted, but after opening it he considered it to be not quite up to the required standard.

Upon investigation the wine proved to be a different year from that stated on the menu and after some animated discussion, with both participants speaking at each other in broken English, the unfortunate waiter was forced to take it away.

Then a new, better variety was offered, accepted, and drunk. And then another and another.

Finally that particular vintage was exhausted and the diners were so drunk that the waiter was able to re-present the original bottle, without complaint.

Later a call came in to the Managing Director from a major customer, a New York trading bank.

The MD had already had a couple of jars before the meal. By the time the call arrived he was too drunk to work his mobile phone and passed it across the table to a colleague.

The phone transfer, like the exchange of a baton in a relay race, failed, and the phone dropped onto the ice bucket. Fortunately it hit the edge and bounced out. The phone was then passed around from person to person until finally a colleague was found who considered himself sober enough to take the call.

The negative tip

A similar scenario developed in an Indian restaurant. On this occasion the meal was completed without incident until the Managing Director presented his credit card to pay the bill. This was before the days of chip and pin. The payment slip, with space for entering a tip and the final total, was passed back to him by the very formal and polite Indian waiter.

With an unsteady hand the Managing Director, who was slightly the worse for wear, entered the sums required, but by some mischance totalled them incorrectly. He had given a negative tip.

The assembled company, in a jolly and uninhibited mood, barracked the unfortunate, polite but unsmiling waiter with loud assurances:

"Nothing personal, mate!".

Breaking glasses

I have heard about this "trick" but never seen it done.

A senior Director, for whom I worked, as a party amusement, would order a pint of beer, drink some of it and then bite a chunk out of the glass, usually (apparently) without injury. He was not much respected for this, however.

Crab claws

The company was going to be sold by the parent group. The directors planned a party to celebrate (after all they had recently awarded themselves long-term contracts).

Everything was booked. Then the deal fell through, but the party would, of course, go on.

It was a tame affair with stale canapés, crab claws, and phoney fish sticks and cheap wine served with little clips that could be attached to the side of the plates to hold the glasses. It came to be known as "the post-non-devolution party".

Eventually the company did change hands, and a further party was held. A director of one of the subsidiaries, a loyal time-server of over thirty years standing, discovered the following morning that he had no written contract of employment, and I guess though sober, no leg to stand on.

The Queen's Award

This is always an excellent opportunity for a really top class party - marquee on the lawn, press coverage, Lord Lieutenant in full regalia, new shirts, ties and dresses.

The factory has been cleaned; the lavatories painted. Films, like those Stalinist ones showing dubious achievements of the Five Year Plan, are shown in the factory.

It is a fine summer's day, but all is not well.

Outside, the front lawn is small. The marquee covers the rose beds which are rather impeding the progress of the visitors, who are in danger of snagging their tights on the roses and sinking their narrow heels into the soft earth.

Cocktails are being served, but some works personnel are feeling neglected. They rightly feel they deserve more recognition as they are the people that have done the real work for very little reward. One of the machinists has decided to roll a barrel of beer under the flap of the marquee and take it back into the factory for later consumption by him and his colleagues.

But, caught on the way, he locks himself into the gents toilet, weeping, and refuses to come out till the party is over.

One office girl, swept off her feet by the freedom of the occasion, a little alcohol and a rookie reporter from the local press, is driven away in an open-topped car, returning some time later with a ripped blouse.

But on the whole it is a good day. Most return home happy and mostly unaware of the emotional turmoil that has gripped some of those around them.

The Queens Award (2)

On the day after the occasion of another such Queen's Award party a colleague of mine awoke to find himself alone on a river bank some five miles from the factory, with no recollection of how he had got there.

Promotion

Have you really arrived?

The joy

On being sent by the group board to visit another industrial company within the group I was surprised to see on their letterhead that I was a Director. No one had told me!

The absurdity of the situation was immediately apparent, but the joy of this new position was, for various reasons, temporary.

One reason was that the company had accepted a huge order for valves for oil pipelines which they could not possibly fulfil, technically, financially or in time.

Wondering what other surprises were in store I prudently decided to "resign".

The last I heard of this company was a call from the panic-stricken and possibly suicidal General Manager, weeping down the phone.

The disappointment

Anticipating the forthcoming retirement of the Managing Director, a highly qualified Deputy MD was appointed, and arrived, full of enthusiasm, and received a warm welcome.

However, it did not take long to become obvious to everyone except the Deputy himself that he was not meeting with favour with the old warhorse of an MD.

Despite his impeccable paper qualifications he was naive, gullible and light-weight.

The word "Deputy" was not, and never could be, deleted nor even changed to "Designate". But, although everyone knew it, no one told him until his final day.

Dodgy dealings

There's little to say about the following anecdotes except that they reveal much about human nature.

The swag bag

During a time of upheaval and unhappiness in the accounts department, Thursday came round and the bag containing thousands of pounds to pay the production workforce was delivered. Shortly afterwards it vanished into thin air. The department's door had been locked as was usual for a Thursday afternoon. No one was accused, uniquely suspected or arrested, but three people left the department shortly afterwards.

The boat

The works was very busy. Overtime was being worked. But output was flagging and the order book was rising. The Production Manager was staying in his office till 1am daily, his face grey with worry and his shoulders with dandruff and cigarette ash. Did he know what was going on? I'm not sure. But everyone else in the works did.

What was happening was that the Technical Director was selling shares in his yacht that was being built from parts made in the factory. Each employee was given shares in the boat according to the number of hours they worked on it.

Meanwhile, of course, the company was paying for the overtime.

This obvious scam went on for some time until the Production Manager and Technical Director both disappeared, leaving the employees with nothing but their basic pay packets, no annual rise and a feeling of growing and justified insecurity.

Back scratching

Every week the chairman came to visit the plant and have lunch in the canteen. While he was there his car was removed, cleaned and filled with fuel.

A tray in the reception office carried a luxurious assortment of whisky, cigars and cigarettes. Mysteriously, this depleted and refilled itself weekly, during his visit.

When I arrived to take over the plant I tried in vain to find out how this feat was accomplished without any receipts being presented or accounts recorded.

I felt I had to put a stop to the tray filling because this part of the scam was blatantly obvious to my staff. The reception goodies stopped, but the remaining activities continued throughout my tenure. I learnt that it was prudent not to say or ask too much.

Helping yourself

On preparing for an exhibition I found that the exhibition boards had police labels on them, identifying them as evidential exhibits. Upon enquiry it turned out that these had been located, amongst other things, at the home of an ex-employee.

The company had pursued an attempt to recover goods they thought he had taken from the stores.

In my suspicious mind I suspected that perhaps the disgruntled employee was owed money by the company and had taken goods in kind to the value of what was owed and that the exhibition boards were just left behind from an earlier exhibition.

Whatever the truth the police did not have enough evidence to prosecute.

Working for yourself

It is very common to find people exploiting a company's difficulties to make a living for themselves. There seems to come a point when they perceive that their efforts would be better served by letting the company go down and then picking up the pieces. Then it is only a small step to helping the company on its way. This what happened in the following case.

A manager had recently been appointed Director. In this new role she was able to see the true state of the company's finances, and she had a personal liability and responsibility. I was a dubious about this lady, an impression perhaps coloured by the knowledge that one of her bras had been found under the seat of the company pool car, but let that pass… The lady was busily advising the company on its future and making plans.

And then it happened, as quick as a flash. The company went down and its remains became a new company of which she and her husband were the two directors.

Concorde

It is remarkable what you can get away with. It is a truism that the greatest rogues are the most plausible. That is the whole point of why it works. There can be few of us that have not been taken in from time to time.

The director of a small company went on a sales trip to the United States.

The duration was three weeks. By a remarkable "coincidence" this was the exact period of the Olympic Games and it was evident on his return that he had attended many of the events. What was more, it soon came to light that he had travelled by Concorde. How could this have been fixed, and who paid? Simple! There was a regional office in Atlanta into which he had placed a colleague with whom he was having an affair, and she was arranging the accounts.

The Wurlitzer

The design office was very busy. The Engineering Director was a prominent local citizen, a popular employer and man of refinement and musical taste.

But his popularity, at least outside the company, was based upon the fact that most of the people in his department were designing new electronic circuits and laying out circuit boards for the Wurlitzer organ in the local theatre, a major project which took several years, all at the expense of the company.

Such tricks don't always work.

The Christmas card

A manager of a company for which I did some work got the company so much into debt through ill-planned and dodgy deals that it became seriously insolvent. The last I heard of him was in a Christmas card from a colleague saying:

"Jim Turner is in prison".

Popeye

Embarrassment is one of the most painful of emotions. I dare say that it lingers in the mind longer than childbirth.

During my first job I was required to take some experimental readings and send the results by fax to an overseas manufacturing plant. This was a task of some early responsibility and I carried it out very diligently and, I thought, with great care. It was only an hour after I had sent the results that I realised that I had placed a decimal point in the wrong place. All the results were out by a factor of ten.

Feeling thoroughly humiliated and embarrassed I owned up and sent a second fax with the simple correction.

Only later did I discover that I was in very good company. The Popeye films based on the strengthening powers of spinach were a result of a similar error. A scientist had overestimated the amount of iron in spinach by a factor of ten in a nutritional study.

When to keep schtum

The red, the blue and the medical

The Group had a strict hierarchy. Group Directors had a red Procedures Manual. Divisional Directors had blue. These manuals covered all sorts of eventualities - whether you could have a saloon, hatchback or estate car, whether you could fly business class to Germany or the USA and so on.

The manuals were loose leaf, so that they could easily be updated, and periodically a pack of new pages would come in the mail with instructions to remove any pages that were superseded. The system was very thorough, but not foolproof - for example there was no difference in paper colour between the versions.

On one occasion I received a pack of papers intended for the red manuals, though I should have had the blue.

It made extremely interesting reading, containing as it did plans for a major reorganisation. In particular it described how the plant at which I worked was to have a new General Manager, a man whom I suspected from talks to some of his former employees to be thoroughly dishonest, quite correctly as it shortly turned out.

What to do with this information?

I decided to say nothing, not even to my wife, and I destroyed the relevant papers. There were several good reasons for this - the planned actions might never happen, and it is best to keep one's powder dry until battle commences. Finally, Group rules said I was not allowed to talk to Group Board Directors except my own, and so it could be very difficult as well as unwise to reveal my hand. But action would be required fairly quickly.

Soon afterwards a memo came down from on high that all Divisional Directors must have a medical. Here was my chance. I refused. This was so unusual that I was requested to go to Head Office to explain myself.

I duly went there and during my meeting with the Group HR Director I was able to explain the reason for my refusal, divulging what I had read and what else I knew. Of course I also agreed to have the medical. The reorganisation never happened.

Buy British

Inconsistency is a trait that we all have, but we don't like it pointed out.

The company chairman decided to institute a "Buy British" policy. Even in those far-off days when you could buy an apparently British-made car there was no saying what you might find if you lifted the bonnet.

The Sales Director took great exception to this policy and told the chairman so. He had some strong arguments. The chairman was keen on brandy and cigars. The Sales Director sincerely hoped that the chairman was purchasing British brandy. Surely those cigars didn't come from Cuba?

The channel tunnel

We are happy to have an "entente cordiale" with our neighbours across the channel. This does not stop a bit of healthy rivalry.

Small talk was being exchanged over luncheon in the board room by the Sales Director of our French distributor, during the period when the channel tunnel was being built. The visitor asked "What do you think of the Channel Tunnel?" to which the Production Director, stopped still with his knife and fork in his hands, and immediately replied:

"I think it's a very good idea. They should fill it with Frenchmen and pull out the plug."

Danger, disillusion and disaster

There are various flavours to this stage in the employment cycle. You can foul up, have someone foul up for you, be betrayed, or misunderstood, or work yourself out of the job, get a vile new boss, or just get bored and fed up.

It is also possible that you were in the wrong job all along - the need to work overcame your native caution, you dummy! (I've done it too…)

A good rule is never to go on holiday for more than two weeks at a time. But even if you obey this rule you can still get caught out.

Jury service

The Production Director was called to jury service. He was allocated a case which lasted three weeks. In the meantime a monthly management meeting took place and his deputy was invited to take part. To everyone's astonishment he told the truth, that is, a quite different story from his boss, who never came back.

Maggots

The worst project I ever had involved checking the rate at which standardised mixtures of household waste would decay and lose moisture in different types of bin. There was a row of bins in my back garden so that I could perform daily checks. This repulsive task required checking weight, smell and other factors.

One Sunday afternoon my wife was enjoying a nap when she was called to the telephone by my client. He had noticed that it was raining at his home. Was it raining at ours? And if so would she (please) mind going outside to check on how the maggots were responding?

Project plans

Project plans are a common part of business life. I'm inclined to say don't make them, or at least don't identify yourself strongly with them or put your personal credibility at stake by publishing them. This is because projects never come in within budget or time scale. Call me an old cynic but you know deep down I'm right. You can provide your own examples.

If you doubt this, remember that anything planned more than 6 months ahead never happens. (Major exceptions are public projects where the published plan is wrong but recovered by throwing your money into it.) The only plan usually needed is a brief outline, and then the work can be detailed 4-6 weeks before action is needed, as the project progresses, when the tasks can be much more clearly seen. This is advice I got from a project manager of a huge contractor designing a North Sea oil rig.

One way of avoiding trouble and avoiding too close identification with a risky project is to put it in the Flashy Ideas Department.

The Flashy Ideas Department

The concept behind this is simple - everyone has bright ideas but not all of them work. This applies equally in the office and at home. Expressing or considering an idea which seems a bit dodgy to you is not in itself a sin, because you may provoke someone else to have a better idea. This is the principle of brainstorming.

But the Flashy Ideas Department takes this principle one stage further. Sometimes an idea is good at the time but goes past its sell-by date. Sometimes an idea escapes to become a real project because someone underestimates the cost and difficulty, or overestimates the market potential.

It is absolutely crucial that such errors are identified and the idea abandoned before it causes real damage. This must be done without loss of face. It is no use throwing good money after bad, or keeping on digging when you are in a pit. It is a bit like my advice on not telling lies - just tell the truth and get it over and done with.

This is why it is necessary to recognise a Flashy Idea for what it is, and allocate it mentally - alone or collectively - to your Flashy Ideas Department and not invest any of your emotional capital in it. This is the only sure and professional way, and one which wins respect in the end.

Who are you with?

When a take-over is in the wind everything slows down except for the Accounts Department. Every prospective purchaser wants a new and up-to-date set of accounts, so the accounts staff are effectively doing a year-end every month. Mysterious visitors walk up and down the open plan office and of course everyone wants to know who they are. It is all very hush-hush at the top, though the rumour mill is going flat out. But it is easy to find out.

A visitor was standing unaccompanied in the office area, which is against company security policy. A member of staff politely asked

"Who are you with?", meaning "Who is accompanying you?" To which the visitor replied "I'm with Hanson Industries".

Swans on the roof

Two of the invariable casualties of the period of uncertainty surrounding a take-over are capital expenditure and maintenance. These can seriously interfere with office efficiency.

In my office, in a new wing of the building, there was a roof leak. The building was settling and water leaked from a slightly different place every day. It was difficult to know where to place my desk. Each morning I came in and moved the desk and the array of buckets. The builder had not been paid and in any case he had what he thought was a cast-iron excuse - there are swans on the roof and they are eating the mastic in the joints!

The twin towers

We all have to take risks - even crossing the road. But it is a good idea to avoid those that are unnecessary.

A few months before 9/11 I was invited by some colleagues to have lunch in the South Tower of the World Trade Centre. After a delicious seafood risotto and a glass or two of white wine, one of them asked me if I would like to take a trip up to the top of the tower. I declined.

See what I mean…?

Buying a car

I had just been offered a much better job. I was in buoyant spirits and decided that I could afford a new car. The buyer of my old firm, to whom I had disclosed this news, suggested that he could get me a car through the firm at a substantial discount. All he had to do was place a company order. He would hide the works copy in his desk so no one would know what he was doing.

Unfortunately there was a delay of six weeks beyond the promised delivery date, by which time I had left the company. The car arrived before I could collect it, and the Works Manager took the call from the garage to say it was waiting for me.

The buyer got the sack, not a good reward for his kindness, a situation for which I was unable to provide a remedy.

The mail shot

The progress, if it can be called that, of the following story was an almost unrivalled demonstration of ineptitude.

Everything was ready. The catalogue was printed and ready for mailing. A covering letter had been written, a date for mailing agreed, 5000 windowed envelopes and reels of pre-paid stamps acquired. A printing company was selected to mail merge the names and addresses onto the letters. To save money it was decided that the office staff would stuff the envelopes by hand.

The Sales and Marketing Director was in charge. Nothing could go wrong, could it? The success of this mailing was vital because the company's business was seasonal. It was absolutely essential that it went out on time.

Returning from a fortnight's leave I was surprised to see that very little had happened while I had been away. More than that, everything that had happened was wrong.

1000 mailers had been posted, it is true. But they had been mailed to the wrong database of existing customers instead of to new prospects, owing to an error by the printer, so the accompanying letter was nonsensical.

No one putting the letters into the envelopes had noticed the error despite their familiarity with the existing customers. They had acted as though on automatic pilot.

Then a new proof copy was prepared by the printer and came into the office for checking. Someone noticed that the addresses did not fit in the window of the envelopes and this was corrected.

Then, because of the delay, the dates within the letter had to be moved forward a month, but there was just still time to get them out. But no one signed off the proof copy.

Several thousand were printed and put into envelopes. At this point it was noticed that the company address block had been printed at the bottom of on the second page instead of on the first page. Also the title of every addressee was wrong.

All the letters had to be reprinted. All the envelopes had to be peeled open and re-filled. They would have to be re-used because they already had stamps on them. But again a proof copy was not signed off.

This time it was noticed, belatedly, that the wrong database had again been given to the printer. This time letters had been printed for territories covered by distributors for which direct sales should not be sought.

Moreover, the letters referred to discounts which could not be afforded in those territories and in any case would seriously undercut the local distributor's prices. The letters all had to be sorted and the offending ones removed.

Now, because of the first mis-mailing, there were no longer enough catalogues printed to fill all the envelopes and complete the task.

Nearly a further month passed before the mailing was finally completed, at least I think it was...

I'm not sure, as I made the strategic decision not to continue in that "organisation".

The sacking

A feeling of danger, especially fear of the sack or redundancy, is not uncommon in a company. The longer you stay in a job the worse it gets because the firm seems to grow in importance while your value in the outside world shrinks both in your own estimation and, if you have not been careful to update your skills and develop varied experience, perhaps in that of certain types of prospective employer. It may even be difficult to obtain job with a competitor – you dare not ask them in case the grapevine goes round and queers your pitch with your present boss.

In reality your firm is a very small operation in relation to the wide world outside, and most of these uncomfortable feelings are unjustified and wasteful of your emotional energy.

They are caused by the very natural and necessary identification with the aims of your employer which enable you to motivate yourself to action.

Sometimes therefore, you work even harder to identify with a useless cause than with a good one, in order to make the task more tolerable. And you may not even be aware that this is what you are doing. Those under you in the organisation whom you try to convince are probably also unbelievers and going through the same agony.

When the company's actions are not in line with your personal views, sheer necessity to keep earning may therefore help you to commit yourself despite your inner feelings, but when you are given tasks which you consider completely barmy, criminal or unethical then it is time to go, or provoke your employer into paying you off.

The good news is that the day after you leave all these anxieties fall away; the old firm shrinks in your mind and will soon appear in a much clearer perspective. However tough the immediate future the world is again your oyster.

Normally, for an employer as well as for the employee, the sacking is the worst part of the job, but it has to be done. Almost always the clues as to what went wrong are present at the recruitment interview. And you will remember the doubts you felt at the time.

If you have to get rid of someone you have personally recruited it is always your fault. The pressure to hire someone, almost anyone, can be great when choice is very limited. But you have forgotten the golden rule "If in doubt, do without".

The first time

The first time I had to sack someone I was particularly anxious. It was a young person who had been taken on as an apprentice before my arrival, and despite his very poor performance I felt that the company had a moral and personal obligation to him, as well as a contract. But his main tasks seemed to be to sweep up and call "Here he comes!" sotto voce from the office corridor and down the stairs into the dirty basement where he and his colleagues worked. There was really no other option than to get rid of him, but I had no idea how the interview would turn out, and had diarrhoea for an hour beforehand.

Later I came to realise that such emotion is unnecessary. Though the pain or resentment of the employee may be real at the time and their pride and self-worth dented, they soon come to realise that something had been wrong all along and that change was needed. And self-justification will overcome self-doubt. Happily, everyone I know who has experienced the sack or been made redundant has fallen on their feet. There's plenty to do in the world.

The drug addict

In my new job I had two bosses, a line manager and a technical director. During my first week I realised that one of my employees was clearly a druggie and was frightening the girls in the office. He had to go.

I went to see my line manager and arranged for a pay-off for the offending employee and we agreed to pay the bill at the local hotel where he was temporarily staying. I then did the dirty deed. It was not long before my other boss rounded on me and the line manager in fury. How dare we do this without consulting him?

It came to light afterwards that the employee was a friend of the technical director, and had been lent money by him. He was also an undischarged bankrupt. Kindness or self-interest had clouded his friend's judgement.

Threatening behaviour

One thing you can't tolerate is violence between employees, at least not in the office.

On one occasion an employee, a highly efficient service engineer, now a director of a major utility, threatened a rather ineffectual production manager with violence if he did not release components needed for an urgent and critical service task in the field. It was a territorial battle over priorities.

I was forced to say to the service engineer that if he did resort to violence I would unfortunately have to sack him immediately.

I did not, of course, say that my regret would be greatly increased by the fact that I would much rather lose the other employee.

The Angel of Death

The events of 9/11 were being felt throughout the company. The New York Office, close to the twin towers, which had been enveloped in impenetrable dust, was closed and would be for six months. Sales had plummeted. It was time to tell me that my interim contract must come to an end. This was not surprising and I had already been making preparations for departure, but the announcement happened in a bizarre way.

The Managing Director, to whom I reported, felt that he should delegate the unpleasant duty of terminating my employment to someone else and appointed the Production Director, whom I knew only slightly and did not report to, to come and see me.

The previous day had been a Sunday, and I had held a great Guy Fawkes bonfire party at home. This had involved doing at least four times as much exercise as in a normal day. I had sawed up a dead tree, dragged it and a huge pile of assorted garden refuse onto the lawn, constructed the bonfire and completely forgotten to have lunch.

Supper went much the same way - there was only time for a couple of pieces of ginger cake with the guests. Then I dashed around tending the bonfire, keeping small people safe and setting off fireworks. It was exhausting but a great success.

The following day, the day planned by the MD for the termination interview, I was physically very tired and undernourished, and when the announcement of my imminent departure was made to me I felt that cold clammy adrenalin feeling and passed out on the office floor.

The first aider was out, and no one else had the sense to raise my legs above my head, which would have revived me quickly. Instead they left me where I lay and called an ambulance. When I awoke, some ten minutes later, the ambulance man was already at my side.

From my responses it was clear that I had had neither a stroke nor a heart attack. No permanent harm had been done to my health. The Production Director, on the other hand, acquired the nickname "The Angel Of Death" for his handling of this case.

At least for a few minutes he really thought that he had killed me.

The photocopier

There was a need for a cost-cutting exercise. This was in the days when a photocopier was the size of a small car and highly unreliable.

At a highly confidential meeting it was decided that the staffing of all departments was to be cut by ten percent.

Of course there was no telling whether you yourself would be among the ten percent at your own level. (Nowadays they have solved that problem by making everyone re-apply for their own job periodically!)

I had made a list of the people I proposed for redundancy and, wishing to keep a copy for my own file, I put my list into the photocopier in the Sales Office. This machine was notoriously unreliable. Two of the secretaries were the only people permitted to open the covers and clear paper jams.

Some red lights came on - it had jammed. But where in the machinery was my piece of paper? Had it got ink on it? That was the big question.

I had to brace myself and tell them that it was highly confidential and not to be looked at as it was removed.

This seemed to work, but of course rumours flourish and the desire to peek at the forbidden is very strong in such situations, so one could never be sure.

The exit interview

The exit interview poses a similar danger to the "reverse appraisal". It's never a good idea to tell people what you think of them, especially your boss. And it matters a lot because the world is very small and one needs friends.

Don't worry

On my last day in a job I was invited into for a meeting with a group director that I had never spoken to before. The meeting seemed pointless - there was nothing to say, and little was said. I bridled when, after a few tense pleasantries, he asked me how old I was. The tone of my factual answer must have made it obvious I felt the question impertinent. His comment was:

"Don't worry, I'm not going to offer you a job."

Eureka!

The same man, on the occasion of a quarterly board meeting visit, had observed one of my employees coming in late. It was relayed to me that I must put this right.

The employee in question, a very talented engineer, but bearded, leather clad and a bit way out, was affronted - his best ideas were often had in the bath - there was no end to the out-of-hours thinking time he spent on the job - I must appreciate that he was there to get the job done not just to be present for the sake of it.

When the same thing happened on the occasion of the next board meeting the stakes were raised. Either I would get him to conform or one or both of us would have to go.

As the employee in question had accumulated a large overdraft and I had no immediate desire to leave, but he now did, he and I agreed that he would be made redundant and given a sum of money sufficient to pay off his creditors. Also he would be allowed time off to find a job, which he did, very quickly.

Enough is enough

Sometimes your last day can creep up on you unexpectedly, despite many clues. The last day can take many forms.

A storekeeper where I worked got so exasperated with unexplained changes of priorities and contrary instructions that he downed tools, tore off his brown coat and jumped on it before leaving for ever by the back door without saying goodbye.

The massage parlour

One manager left a company that I used to work in. At his next new employment he was seen visiting a gay massage parlour in works time. He was dismissed and decided to contest the matter. When the case finally came to court he claimed he was visiting the establishment on account of a bad back, and was awarded a 6-figure sum for unfair dismissal on these grounds and that the company had not gone through a proper disciplinary procedure.

The company is going, too

When working as a consultant I visited a company to be greeted by a worried-looking director. He could not give me much time as they were to have an emergency board meeting. A few minutes later he emerged white as a sheet to announce that the company was going into liquidation. I put my arms around him to support him while he tried to come to terms with the situation.

As well as being sympathetic I had quickly to assess my own position. As my fee was being paid by a government department we agreed that I would write a summary of the work done to date and raise an invoice which he would sign before I left. And this we did.

From notices sent out by the receiver over the coming months it emerged that the company had never in fact been insolvent - instead there had been a major foul-up in the accounts and the stock records.

The wasp sting

While I was going through that unenviable task of giving someone the sack the conversation was extending longer than was comfortable or necessary. I was keen to terminate the interview when I was conveniently interrupted by the ringing of the telephone.

It was my wife on the line. A wasp had gone up her skirt and stung her twice on a tender part. This provided the ideal cue.

A tearful parting

A long-serving senior member of staff was moving on to better things. As well as being a valued employee he was also a family friend. A card was sent round, money collected and a present bought and wrapped. On the final day we gathered in the office and it was my task to hand over the present and give him a warm send-off.

Facing the gathering of staff I made a short speech and turned to the leaver, only to find that my words had been so moving that he had burst into tears.

The Last Post

My own most moving exit was when I working in a very junior capacity in a research lab. My technician had learnt to play the bugle at the Pangbourne Naval College. He brought it in and played "The Last Post" in the works car park.

A board meeting was being held in the board room overlooking the car park and I felt, maybe somewhat ridiculously, that a communal feeling of regret and loss was being felt by all. It was very moving.

Postscript

Where do we go from here?

Having looked back over some of the many incidents of my working life I feel that I have now done with British industry, or it has done with me, or perhaps it is now crying out for your help, energy and enthusiasm.

Human nature can be a source of both joy and misery. But there is no place either for self-justification or despair. I seek instead a middle road - realism, the enjoyment of love and sunshine, satisfaction in what I do and the pleasures of friendship.

You will have to work out your own way of surviving, enjoying life and staying sane. I hope this book will help.

I've said little about the things that I worked on. I think they would be boring to you. They were just part of my individual survival plan.

You will have your own adventure, your own trajectory through life. But I'm sure that like me, even if you can't change the whole world, you can do some good to those around you, most of the time.

May you be rewarded with the satisfaction of that knowledge.

AN ANTHOLOGY OF
CONTEMPORARY ROMANIAN
POETRY

For Margareta Dobrescu

AN ANTHOLOGY OF
CONTEMPORARY
ROMANIAN
POETRY

TRANSLATED

BY

ANDREA DELETANT
and
BRENDA WALKER

FOREST BOOKS
LONDON * 1984 * BOSTON

Published by FOREST BOOKS
20 Forest View, Chingford, London E4 7AY, U.K.
61 Lincoln Road, Wayland, MA. 01778, U.S.A.

First published 1984

Typeset in Great Britain by Cover to Cover, Cambridge
Printed in Great Britain by A. Wheaton & Co. Ltd., Exeter

Jacket design © Ann Evans
Translations © Andrea Deletant, Brenda Walker

British Library Cataloguing in Publication Data
1. Romanian poetry – Translations into English.
2. English poetry – Translations from Romanian.
I. Deletant, Andrea   II. Walker, Brenda
859'.134'08   PC871.E3
ISBN 0-950948-74-8

Library of Congress Catalog Card Number 84-81308

Cover photograph:
Sculpture
PRAYER
Constantin Brâncuşi 1876–1957
1907/bronze/Art Museum of the Socialist Republic of Romania. Bucharest.

Contents

Preface

Romanian is a Romance language that developed almost two thousand years ago from Latin, then spoken in the region of the lower Danube, and the Romanians today are the only East European people to speak such a language. Grammatically, Romanian differs from the other Romance languages (French, Portuguese, Italian, and Spanish) by preserving a case system and by suffixing the definite article. Although its vocabulary is essentially of Latin origin, Romanian has also been influenced at various times by Slavonic, Greek and Turkish. The spoken rhythms, however, remain notably iambic, which facilitates a close translation of Romanian poetry into English.

In his recent anthology of Romanian Poetry (Editura Eminescu, Bucharest, 1982) Dan Duțescu points out that:

"The so-called outward trimmings of poetry – rhythms, rhyme, alliteration, assonance, as well as onomatopoeia – are not, when we have to do with true poetry, mere additions, mere tags, trinkets and trimmings and trappings and tinkling bells, but the substance and grain of poetic matter itself."

In this anthology, we have attempted to retain the substance and grain within each poet's individual style.

While poets in Romania do not always admit to being influenced by each other, they do admit to the influence of their "Last Romantic"[1], Mihail Eminescu (1850–1889) whose importance for Romanian literature they liken to that of Shakespeare and Chaucer in English literature. Eminescu, with themes drawn from the past, from Romanian folk literature and from his own experience, and expressed in a language enriched by the use of archaisms and the adoption of neologisms, raised Romanian verse to new heights.

At the turn of the century, some Romanian poets experimented with the techniques of symbolism. The verse of George Bacovia (1881–1957) is distinguished by its musicality, its use of mood colours and a repetition of key words, which highlights the monotony and pessimism of his interior contemplation.[2] His contemporaries Tudor Arghezi, Ion Barbu, Lucian Blaga and Vasile Voiculescu gave Romanian poetry its golden age. Arghezi's prosodic innovation and rugged metaphor introduced a new dimension, but it is Blaga, with his philosophic verse, often expressed in symbols and myths, to whom many contemporary poets acknowledge a debt.

The postwar Stalinist era was a period of literary sterility. A number of poets, such as Nina Cassian, commenced writing at this time, but others, such as Ştefan Augustin Doinaş, were unable to publish until the mid-sixties. Those who had established themselves before the war ceased to be acknowledged officially.

However, the release in 1964 of thousands of political prisoners signalled the relaxation of the Romanian régime's rigidity and this was rapidly reflected in the country's cultural life. Barbu, Blaga and Voiculescu were posthumously rehabilitated. Censorship became less strict allowing a sudden blossoming of new literature in which a group of young poets emerged. Among them were Ioan Alexandru, Ana Blandiana, Constanţa Buzea, Nichita Stănescu (who died at the age of fifty in December 1983) and Marian Sorescu. Up to the present time, this group of poets has remained the most widely read and respected by public and critics alike. Their styles are very different, yet each of the poets in his or her own way reflects the "anguish of being".

Marin Sorescu's humorous, yet cogent irony, and anecdotal characters set his style apart from the more ornate, ambiguous or intellectual poetry of many of his contemporaries. His style is characterised by an unexpected and ironic substitution for the predicted conclusion of a colloquial phrase.

Ana Blandiana shares Ioan Alexandru's stark dramatic vision and spiritual qualities, but she also expresses an affinity with nature, where hair can "take root", or backs grow together like "two branches". Her sensitivity for the human condition is reflected not only in "The Couple" and "Torquato Tasso", but also in her latest poems "Courage", "Outburst" and "Suspicion".

Ioan Alexandru's spirituality is rural, portraying ancient rituals, the destiny of "his village" being linked to that of the cosmos. His dramatic skill and ear for dialogue is well exemplified in such ironic portrayals as "The End of the War".

A vein of anxiety permeates Nina Cassian's poetry. There is a strong presence of a destructive force, often felt first in nature, as in her poem "Dank Steps". However, her more sententious poems encapsulate moments of everyday experience common to all.

Constanţa Buzea's melodious verse poignantly reflects human relationships and the bitter taste left by loneliness.

It is said of Ştefan Augustin Doinaş that he puts form before emotion, portraying a "post romantic classicism". Our selection reflects his intellectual rigour and an equilibrium between expression and lyricism.

In many of the later poems of Nichita Stănescu there is an obsession with death. His self-irony and surrealistic imagery often related to animism offer a vision of a single life in which all take part.

Since the early 1970s there has been a wealth of new poetry, from which we have selected six poems by Ion Stoica. His lyricism owes a debt to Blaga, yet he has an originality which produces a fluidity of movement through time and space, fusing thought with feeling.

Our aim in this anthology is to introduce the reader to the work of several of the most significant contemporary Romanian poets. In a future volume we hope to provide a wider selection of 20th century Romanian verse. Most of the poems here, as far as we are aware, have not been previously translated into English.

A special word of thanks is owed to all those who have encouraged us in this undertaking.

Andrea Deletant
Brenda Walker

[1] *The Last Romantic*, Roy MacGregor-Hastie, University of Iowa Press, 1972.
[2] *Plumb/Lead*, George Bacovia, Translated by Peter Jay, Foreword by Marian Popa, Minerva Publishing House, Bucharest, 1980.

Acknowledgments

Poems in this anthology have been taken from the following volumes:

Ioan Alexandru
Poeme 1970 (Editura Eminescu, Bucureşti)

Ana Blandiana
Cincizeci De Poeme 1970 (Editura Eminescu, Bucureşti)
Octombrie, Noiembrie, Decembrie 1972
(Editura Cartea Românească, Bucureşti)
Somnul Din Somn 1977 (Editura Cartea Românească, Bucureşti)
Ora De Nisip 1983 (Editura Eminescu, Bucureşti)

Constanţa Buzea
Poeme 1977 (Editura Albatros, Bucureşti)

Nina Cassian
De Indurare 1981 (Editura Eminescu, Bucureşti)

Ştefan Aug. Doinaş
Alfabet Poetic 1978 (Editura Minerva, Bucureşti)

Marin Sorescu
Poeme 1965 (Editura Pentru Literatura, Bucureşti)
Moartea Ceasului 1966 (Editura Tineretului, Bucureşti)
Tuşiţi 1970 (Editura Eminescu, Bucureşti)
Fîntîni In Mare 1982 (Editura Eminescu, Bucureşti)

Nichita Stănescu
Epica Magna 1978 (Editura Junimea, Iaşi)

Ion Stoica
Porţile Clipei 1982 (Editura Albatros, Bucureşti)

Ioan Alexandru
(b. 1941)

IMAGE

I see my father holding a huge loaf in his arms
by the light of the lamp.
For the little sister he cuts a little slice,
for the larger boy, he cuts a larger slice,
for the biggest brother, the biggest slice,
and Mama's left to cut her own in her corner
near the hearth where night's already fallen,

and then time appears, a powerful whirlwind,
no one can stand aside.
In the middle of the house on the face of that earth,
three paths appear chiselled in stone,
different, full of smoke and sweat falls —
and rusted chill.

The crumbling roof breaks
and damp leaves fall in the corner of the lane
and one autumn morning
a boy rises to the sky
and all the village is lit by his image
as by a new planet.
And graves in the earth widen
where greying ages withdraw
for eternity of the snows.

THE END OF THE WAR

When I come into the world war were endin',
Last orders were shot. On field
Last canons were hung by their shadows.
In our house presents were shared.

'First to you, John,' said the War to father, from the corner of the
                                    table,
'Because you have served me faithfully,
I hand you this wooden leg.
Wear it in memory of me, and good health to you.
It's sturdy from the trunk of an old oak;
When you die the woods will rock you
Like a brother in the summits of their eyes.
Your right hand, because it has no book learning anyway,
I wrenched from your elbow and have given it to the earth
To teach it to write.

'For you, Maria,' said the War to mother –
'Because you watered my horses with your tears
And left two sons on the battlefield
To polish my boots, and brought up
Two maidens with whom I've spent my nights,
Look, I'll give you this beautiful bunch of white hair
To adorn your temples
And this even bigger bunch of wakeful nights,
As well as this empty house without a roof.

To you, George, son of Peter from over the hill, –
For the two hazel eyes, you say you had,
Look, I give you possession of all the boundaries of darkness,
So you can harvest them, you and your wife
Forever.

For the village, I leave only forty orphans
Under six months, ten empty houses and the others in ruins,
Also, the sky towards sunset, half burned.
The tower without bells; eight women in the cemetery
Hung with heads to the ground, and twenty horses dead from the
                                 neighbour's farm.

For you, just born, because anyway we don't know each other very
                                                            well,
I leave the cows udder dry,
The plum trees burned alive in the garden,
The eye of the well, dead,
And may the sky feed you on its stars.
And I baptize you in the name of the Lord.

APPARITION

In rain crammed on the sea,
in a broken hut
we prepared for the journey to earth.
Long lightning all the night,
waters groaned in grey whirlpools,
and putrid planks creaked underfoot.
Alone and without sleep,
when the crucified one on the cross, alive, bleeding,
appeared over us. We huddled in awe,
what were we hoping? When his arms were heard blasting
in our breast. Were we burning? Were we sleeping?
Or had we died long ago?
The cross and pale beard disappeared in the deep
pulled by heavenly ropes towards immortal horizons.

AS IN PARADISE

Our cemetery is common land
surrounded by a stone fence,
so as not to be caught by earth
left alive in liberty.

The wooden crosses, after a few years
lean on one side and then also die
forever, and strange men come
on wild mares and steal them
for their fires.

The plot of the grave is wiped away –
wiry grass clutters everywhere
like hair on heads of the young on winter nights;
when the cemetery is full to the brim from one end
to the other, everything starts again from the beginning;
the grave of my grandfather is on the grave of my great
                                        grandfather,
my father over my grandfather,
and likewise the old mayor
over the age-old mayor– the old priest
over the age-old priest,
the old village over the ancient village.

At the edges grow plum and apple trees
And scented flowers can be seen,
their vapour penetrates into things
far away.
Those who come passing by here
with watches buried in their left wrist
and shoulders full of old age
marvel as in paradise.

JOB

After Job lost his last son
He began to convince himself that from now on death
Was his only companion. So near he drew to it
And gradually confessed to it, that for Job another life began.
The one without risk, without advice, without hope,
Without the simplest longing, without repentance,
Without blemish. Faith was no longer a fortress
To be conquered by devotion.
He lost all sense of action, all sense of temptation,
For some time then the flesh on his body had left him.
His eyes turned in upon himself, hands motionless. –
Job was passing into the other world without any regret,
Without any knowledge,
Just as were born and died the dead
Before the birth of God.

MY SISTER

None of you who are my age
can know my elder sister,
nor do I know her other than from sleep
and oblivion.
In hazy weather in the long lost autumn,
she died before I was born
and so hurried my coming
to that empty place left in the world.
That's why I'm also taller,
grown in her shade,
and have reached more quickly the age of doubt.

I'm preparing for autumn in full spring
and in summer I hear the frost of winter in my bones,
I carry through the world my sister's void,
When I die, I'll have been dead a long time.

Ana Blandiana
(b. 1942)

A VILLAGE

More of a smell
Than image or sound,
The smell of smoke in the evening,
Especially when the herds return, dizzy
From too much milk flowered in the fields;
Smell of milk making a froth,
Pulled erotically from the udder, as if
Coupling in its blue flesh
The green soul of wild grass
With the gentle, moving
Breath of smoke;
The smell of wet straw
And heaps of berries,
Smell of wheat pyramids rising to the sky,
While the air of evening seeps back into itself
And clouds unfold
Into brief stories and vanish;
The smell of self,
Of hair long in the sun,
Of skin for herbs dreaming,
Of sleep and of word –
A village built on air
From endless seeming,
Loved with one's breath
And rocked by the wind!

A MEETING

Don't be afraid.
Everything will be so easy
That you won't even understand
Until much later.
You will wait at the beginning
And only when
You begin to believe
That I don't love you anymore
Will it be hard for you,
But then I will make
A blade of grass grow
In our corner of the garden,
To reach out
And whisper:
Don't be afraid,
She's fine
And waiting for you
Near these roots of mine.

TORQUATO TASSO[1]

He came from the darkness towards me, the poet,
The poet who failed because of fear.
He was very handsome. As on an X-ray
You could see the poetry on his body,
Poetry unwritten through fear.
"I am mad" – he said. A fact I knew
From the foreword to his books.
But like a password he carried his madness
To enter here, as if he would say
"I redeem myself thus
For in my poems there's lack of truth.
The price is immense. I approach you. Receive me!"
But I answered: Go away from here!

"I wrote at the flames of the Inquisition" – he told me –
"Feeling on my body
The hair shirt singeing.
My room had monks' eyes for windows
And their ears stuck to each other, for doors,
And mice coming out of their holes were monks,
And at night huge birds wore habits to sing to me.
You must understand . . ." And with a finger he pointed
Showing in my body the poetry there,
The unwritten poetry . . .
But I shouted: Go away from here!

[1] Italian poet (1544–1595) who died on the brink of insanity.

WEARINESS

What unassuming dead we have!
Through volcanoes they've never erupted,
Even with walls built upon them
They do not stir.
With gestures carved by others
They let themselves be held in statues,
They let flags be harnessed to them
On unknown roads,
They let themselves be ploughed and dutifully rot
To feed the earth
What unassuming dead we have
And wearied.

DO YOU REMEMBER THE BEACH?

Covered with painful fragments
Do you remember the beach
On which
We couldn't walk barefoot,
The way
You were looking at the sea
And saying you were listening to me?
Do you remember
The frantic seagulls
Wheeling in the ringing
Of unseen church bells
Whose patrons were fishes,
And how
You distanced yourself running
Towards the sea
Calling to me
That you needed distance
To look at me?
The snow
Was dying
Stirred with the birds
In the water,
With an almost happy despair
I was watching
The prints of your steps on the sea
And the sea
Was closing like an eyelid
Over the eye in which I waited.

FALLING ASLEEP

I fall asleep, you fall asleep,
The way we stay with eyes closed
Stretched next to each other
We seem two youths equally dead.
Listen how sleepily rustles the sun
Through the dried grasses,
The sky is soft and leaves on the fingers
A sort of pollen.
Over our faces move
The shadows of flocks of birds,
The smell of grapes seeps into us.
Fall asleep,
Don't be afraid,
Our neighbouring hair strands
Spread on the grass
Have begun to take root,
Soon the leaves will cover us
In the golden snow.
We've never looked more alike,
Your wings have sunk into the earth
And cannot be seen any more.

KEEP YOUR EYES CLOSED

Keep your eyes closed,
Keep your eyes closed,
It's only given to us once,
I ask you nothing
The snow settles down.
It's buried the cemetery and the village
It's walling up the church,
Tops of poplars can still be seen above
Like grass growing.
The snow settles and leavens
As a field fermenting
Which will soon stop
The time from above falling.
Keep your eyes closed
It's only given to us once
And only once must we give.
I ask you nothing, only
Wait for the last time-flake to set
And void becomes the sky,
And in silence, only then
Unfold your left arm from the nails
And send the snow-glass gently turning.

ASLEEP

Asleep
I happen to cry out,
Only when asleep,
And frightened by my own daring
I wake,
In the well disciplined silence of night,
And try to hear
Cries from neighbours' sleep.
But the neighbours are wise
Crying out only when they're sure
That they dream they're asleep.
In the sleep within sleep
Where no one can hear,
They give way to cries.
What free uproar
Must be there,
In the sleep within sleep.

A COUPLE

Some only see you,
Others see only me,
We superimpose so perfectly
That no-one can spot us at the same time
And no-one dares to live on the edge
From where we can both be seen.
You only see the moon,
Only I see the sun,
You yearn for the sun,
I yearn for the moon,
But we stay back to back,
Bones united long ago,
Our blood carries rumours
From one heart to the other.
What are you like?
If I lift my arm
And stretch backwards
I discover your sweet shoulder-blade
And, going upwards, the fingers touch
Your divine lips,
Then suddenly return
To crush my mouth, bleeding.
What are we like?
We have four arms for defence
But only I can hit the enemy here
And only you the enemy there,
We have four legs to run,
But you can only run on your side
And I on mine.
Every step's a life and death struggle.
How equal are we?
Are we to die together or will one of us carry,
For a time
The corpse of the other stuck to our side
Infecting with death, slowly, too slowly,
Or perhaps never to die completely
But carry for an eternity
The sweet burden of the other,
Atrophied forever,

The size of a hunch,
The size of a wart . . .
Oh, only we know the longing
To look into each other's eyes
And so at last understand,
But we stay back to back,
Grown like two branches
And if one should tear away,
Sacrificing all for a single look,
You would only see of the other
The back from which you came
Bleeding, shivering,
Tearing.

WHEN I'M ALIVE

When I'm alive in my dream
On earth I've died
And when I'm still here
Am I dead inside?

Or is it only a game
With a moon and sun
Who sadistically share me
Ruling as one?

When it's night here
In sleep it's light –
I come back unwilling
From dream and from life.

IT'S SNOWING

It's snowing with malice,
The snow falls with hate
Above waters icy with loathing,
Above orchards blossomed by evil,
Above embittered birds who suffer,
It snows as if the acquatic dweller
Would feel this life ebbing,
It snows
With human drive, –
Venomously it's snowing.
Who then to surprise?
Only I know
That once a flurry of snow
Was love, at the beginning. –
It's so late
And hideously it's snowing,
And my mind's stopped working
So I wait
For it to be of use
This wolf that's starving.

IN THE MORNING AFTER DEATH

In the morning after death
It will be cold as in the misty dawns of September,
When from the lustful scorching heat of summer
I come round in the white air,
A stranger to the trees, light entangled, woollen,
I will be woken, as in September, early
And, as in September,
Alone enough to hear
The air as it drips towards noontime
On the cheek of wet quinces.
And I will be tired,
And beg to stay asleep,
A little longer,
Lying without motion,
With eyes closed, face to the cushion,
While the deafening silence
Will awake me more and more,
To begin,
Like a morning in autumn,
Eternal daytime.

ONLY WITH ME

Only with me
And so reconciled
Under the last sun,
Almost faded in the orchard
So that I can hear
The colours in the leaves flowing
And the gentle rustling
Of the soft clouds.
Only with me.
Such a good silence.
Nothing to say.

SO COLD

So cold that saliva freezes
On dogs' teeth
While they howl to the moon
Going mad with fear.
So cold my lips tear
With terror when I shout
And with the blood, still warm,
I lick it like a beast.

A CHURCH FULL OF
BUTTERFLIES

A church full of butterflies,
Icons dusty with pollen,
Drowned in a silence poisoned
By slow movement of wings
Deep and rhythmic;
A church in which
Antennae
Cringe at the tips
Blindly touching the altar,
While the light
The crumbly light tumbles
Above the ambiguous rustle
Of cloaks of saints
And wings . . .
I sit in the pew rigid
Terrified their flight
May touch me,
Understanding why I know everything –
I made the clumsy drawing
On the wings
In my childhood,
When I first learned to write,
The church much later,
Forgetting,
On the same paper . . .

PIETA

The clear pain, the death has brought me back,
Submitted to your arms, almost a child.
You don't know whether to be thankful
Or cry
For such happiness,
Mother.
My body, stripped of the mystery
Is yours alone.
Sweet your tears drip onto my shoulder
And gather obediently near the blade.
How good it is!
The pilgrimages and words never to be understood,
The disciples, of whom you're proud, of whom you are afraid,
The Father, the assumed, the unspoken, watching,
All is behind.
Calmed by the understood suffering
You hold me in your arms
And stealthily
You rock me, gently,
Rock me, Mama.
Three days only, I'm allowed to rest
In death and on your lap.
Then the resurrection will come
And again you are not meant to understand.
Three days only,
But until then
I feel so good
On your lap, descended from the cross,
If I wasn't afraid you'd find it terrifying,
Gently I'd turn my mouth
To your breast, suckling.

SO SIMPLE

Oh, if only I were a candle,
To waste gradually
From one end to the other,
Simply, as in sums
Of children . . .
My mind first – what happiness! –
Would disappear.
People would say
"How mindless is this girl!"
I'd remember nothing
Nor attempt to understand.
My heart would then melt
And I'd love no more,
Hate no more,
No suffering would reach me,
And people would say
"How heartless is this girl!"
And again, again
And then not one wish more
No passion,
And my blood, carrier of ships
Would scatter,
To leave only
Shrivelled knees,
Shaking with dignity or kneeling.
No one would even speak.
In the last silence,
The wax pool
Especially punished, cooled
For the horrific shadows which
Its light brought into the world.

WINGS

Churches don't have roofs,
But wings shivering on bodies
Of wooden tiles,
Soon the time will come
For them to open
And rise
Slowly, as if reluctantly,
Carrying their beings
Of gold and smoke
Into the air higher and higher,
Flying with great roaring, like
A flock of heavy birds
Towards sunset,
While the mountains, in panic,
Mixed with sea
Rushing towards them
Would unfurl –
For the world a beautiful ending
Under the life blue sky
Swarming with great churches
Living.

SUSPICION

Does the flower have liberty
When everything's fixed,
The precise date
When it blooms and dies,
The smell
It's supposed to emit
And the colour which sets it alight?
It says yes.
And the petals say yes, each in turn,
And the stamins, and pollen grains,
And the leaves and the thin, fragile
Stems. Yes.
But what then is liberty? I ask
A little embarrassed by suspicion of the reply
What a question! amazed,
The angel blinked his petals.

SOOT

What do you think about when you see
An archangel covered in soot?
Of the pollution of the stratosphere, of course.
And what else?
Of the habit of angels
To find their way into everything.
And what else?
Of the chimney in spring beginning
To smoke and get clogged-up.
And what else?
Oh, if I think hard,
An archangel covered in soot
Could also be an archangel who
Set himself on fire
Forgetting he couldn't burn.

OUTBURST

At each outburst
A god unfolds
Blowing large folds
Of his cloak across the sky.
There are so many kinds of gods
On earth
That we'll never be able
To laugh or cry enough
To entice them from where they hide.
Whether laughter or tears,
It doesn't really matter:
Important is the outburst.

COURAGE

I'm looking at my hands:
Little fronds where
Eyelids of leaves
Never blink;
Tips of wings where
Feathers haven't dared
To increase;
And at the ends,
Not even claws have been able
To spring up as
Gentle buds of a beast.
I look at my hands
As I would at letters
Which haven't the courage
To make themselves.
Into a word.

Constanţa Buzea

(b. 1942)

THERE WHERE I THINK YOU ARE

There where I think you are,
Not even trains pass,
The forests of frosty firs
Appear there like glass.

Further and further away you feel,
Always added to the rest, and still.
I cannot go forward
Unless I lose myself as well.

And all time breathes white,
White are roads in the snow,
I wouldn't even recognise you now
Without the pair of us, without a halo.

I feel pity when remembering,
Yet can't bring myself to forget
How much illusion is in destiny,
How many mistakes can be met.

As if from under a snowed up shawl
With cold fingers I gather
Our soul, still sincere,
With its movement towards silver.

The way it snows, it may not stop,
And the firs would be encircled there,
Amongst barbarian meteorites,
There where I think you are.

Every year I wait
For the snow, so that I can see you,
See if you look, if you listen,
If you understand a little more now.

THE NAIVE REWARDING OF ONE WHO LIES

The same old journeys and the same old aims,
The same old pigeons on a bowl of lentils,
The naive rewarding of the one who lies.

I'm longing for rest and for holy things,
For full and bitter tears,
For humility and for prayers
Towards the sadness of mothers' graves.

Because few words I'm saddled with,
They're hung round my neck, and my mind demands
An eye for an eye, and a tooth for a tooth.

SPEAK WELL OF ME

Speak well of me, to those who trespass against me.
Into my own soul I fall as in a pit
Whenever I stay lying down in grass near water
Like a death it's afraid of me.

In my dream grazes a white herd,
And autumn appears the same everywhere.
I entrust you with this empty page
So earth will not know how I fared.

Whenever longing is longer than death,
I see before me rings of danger,
My inside betrays me, we cannot be alone,

As far as I can see, a wall of eyes.
It is made insatiable, wildly beautiful
The scene that comes towards home.

THE END OF THE WORLD

Don't let memory keep
All the words,
Our hurtful words,
Beautiful and cold.

Chosen and calmly spoken,
You hardly understand them,
Our hurtful words,
When they leave, you bury them.

There is silver and shadows of kings
At the end of the world,
Our hurtful words,
Beautiful and cold.

THE SIN OF PRIDE

The trees shake great birds,
And the vineyards Divine nectar.
The way to me is far,
The way to death is nearer.

I get up every autumn,
It seems a path I can't remember.
The way to me is far,
The way to death is nearer.

These words for harvesting
I feel as desires, yet I know I'm to suffer,
All my love came true
And proved so right for its future.

Why aren't I, as it would appear,
In decline, unhappier!
The way to me is far,
The way to death is nearer.

LOCKED IN THE
ADULT WORLD

Stay a child, yet think
While locked in the adult world.
Stay a child, shyly passing
And listening to words.

If for everyone the wind is blowing,
For you it has a special meaning,
A feeling of immortality.

Be pure, hiding
From others who are sinning,
Be sorry for the clouds,
And for them changing,
For which they're not guilty.

Nina Cassian
(b. 1924)

THAT'S ABOUT IT

More and more often,
more and more painfully,
I remember something else:
how a child once pulled faces at me,
how all the addresses where I lived
had names of plants,
the smell of my drawing book
and, after that,
the atmosphere of a kiss which embraced me,
kisses to suffocation I walked and breathed,
and, after that, sacks with the dead
which I carried on my back
and still carry
—well, yes, that's about it,
that would be about it
this is what you'd call my life,
the one in the skin of the sea,
in the garment of the grass,
in the curse of not speaking,
in the labour of not creating.

LIKE ANA

Once I entered with you
into a house of love
and left it fleeing
from misunderstanding,
hating the long street
and the sky with stars.
Then fell the first stone
on my heart.
Now the building is completed.
No more breathing from anyone inside.

DANK STEPS

Spring – a girl on crutches
with cheeks sharp and grey
as an icicle of dirty water
hits dogs and trees
with her crutches
and curses like an old crone.
Windows have wrinkles
and there's heavy thunder.
Spring – a girl
with hair of mud
shapes in mud
human forms
with her crutches.

MORNING EXERCISES

I wake up and say: I'm through.
It's my first thought at dawn.
What a nice way to start the day
with such a murderous thought.

God, take pity on me
– is the second thought, and then
I get out of bed
and live as if
nothing had been said.

WITHOUT GUILT

You don't have to be guilty
to suffer punishment.
Look what happened to the flower!
It had just appeared, pink among leaves,
and the big animal came
and blew an insult all over it.

DOWNHILL

How minute we are.
How hurried we are.
How coarsely we speak.
Only the spider
stayed all night in the same place
on the side of the bath.
– Good morning, eight-legged patient one,
silent witness.

We decline, deteriorate,
when the supreme criteria degenerate.

HORIZON

And yet there must exist
a zone of salvation.
Sad are the countries
who don't have outlets to water,
dull are the people who have no outlet from themselves
toward another outlet, even greater.

OPTICAL ILLUSION

In perfect darkness,
without moon, without lights, without fireflies,
without there, without here,
– a complete peace,
a complete stillness
of black on blackness.

PRESSURES

If the tear
is the egg of the rain bird
if the bird is air full of unease
which itself
is a body over bodies
– how can I write a book
in this communal grave?

IF I HAD DIED IN AN EARTHQUAKE

Who do you want to carry in your arms?
I was a little girl, I was a little boy.
I left childhood
with too large a head,
and entered youth with too small a shoulder.

And when I reached proportions of gold,
a tremor came
a tremor of lead
– why mention it . . .

The poet said: I'm a beautiful memory.

ECHO

Yesterday, I heard again the crashing fall
of the house of the world
and in the silence that followed
I again felt full of awe.

A promiscuous death,
has mingled
life with no life,
something glitters, it's not known
whether it's a needle
or a splinter from my bone.

Ştefan Aug. Doinaş
(b. 1922)

INVOCATION TO NIGHT

Spherical is reality.
At noon dangling,
my eye weeping
darkness for a country.

Only the wide-eyed owl
confirms it, eerily,
his iris ethereally,
keeps it under seal.

Night, possess me!
A thousand things and deeds,
lightning without pity

like stars in a bunch
in my pupil revolving,
smoking it with significance.

LIFE BURNS AWAY AT EITHER END

What is the wisdom of a book compared to the wisdom of an angel?

Hölderlin

Life burns away at either end, with a difference.
   We're only just born, and the divine is in us
      still feeling its way in play, when – look:
         a jungle is now the paradise about us and

only with nails like sickles, only
      with beaks and jaws can salvation be caught
         in flight. Middle-age is hunting,
            and like beasts is hunted daily.

Then, comes enlightened rest,
    when bones still hold
        the evening sun above the plain,
           and the odour of the pale stubble field.

Yes! But who rides the stallion
    now and writes with the iron of the plough?
        Whose grey footwear is
           dusted with smiles, with strands of hair?

Greying angels among suckling ones,
    the divine surrounds us and we play again
        the first game but with hollow beads,
           our gains deducted from losses.

Is this the way we'll sip wisdom?
    Yet how can we taste it, if we haven't left
        souls in the hilts of our swords
           and our mouths on the mouth of the mad?

Life burns away at either end, with a difference,
    for in the evening, when we put out the children with tales,
        the deed they hear is the fire of innocence,
           but the mouth that tells it is ash.

THE WORDS OF THE POET

As birds rise in the skies leaving an empty straw nest
searching for a king of birds, each beady-eyed,
and then day by day above the world the meeting is delayed
until, sensing the flock their loving king, end their quest

so words start searching for that essential instant
which bathes the pulse in moments of brilliance and perpetuity
words more than ever alien as an unendured austerity
divided by potential speech and ever more obedient

until the white page digests them like clusters settling
in which the dead deed blows coolly from meaning.

THE KISS

Like the leaf which floats to the well
I trouble your soul for a kiss,
and your mouth gulping me, stirs
with waves whose needs you can't tell.

Nor does the fire more strongly shudder
nor does the breeze get you drunk any easier.
The leaves on your shoulder, a crackling shower
which fall from a single song.

Why are you sighing? Which cloud enters you?
On your beauty, like waves above you
comes down, lazily, a shadowy shawl.

Ah! On the lips my leaf to ashes is turning . . .
But, the wild vein, rotting,
scratches its image in the soil.

THE NIGHT

We knew it was coming: the mud in the lakes
was turning pink, only the trill
of fading birds still floated in air,
and smoke was rising with an ever
open palm – to receive it; water
was talking to itself near rocks.

We were still together. Simple space
created only with breath, a step
in which begins the furnace.
I held the first star in my right hand,
but only the hand knew it, the gaze
on two paws – waiting for it to arrive.

It oozed gently: with scarabs,
which were beginning to melt in air,
with your eyes, in which our place
was receiving someone strange, and with grass,
where it was forever night.

SEPTEMBER

Silver knife through the gorged heart
of September. Melodiously
travels the sound of brass, and then starts
to go down a semitone, suddenly.
But what light still! . . . Avid wasps
besiege the sweetness: sparkles
on the surface of a sphere which grasps
emptiness of night in its superb wealth.
Will we exist – or not? A mystical feast
of upturned flight is offered us on the wind:
as it is the apple, while setting light
to distance between branch and earth . . .

Marin Sorescu
(b. 1936)

THE TRAVELLER

In memory, the waters I've just come through
Have left a slight sheen under the skin,
I can't run agilely with speed
Unless I have heels covered in blisters,
Unless they feel like a marsh,
Where you sink, imperceptibly.

I can only fall asleep when I crouch
Somewhere on a suitcase near overcrowded
Train doors,
Woken from dozing everytime a passenger gets on
Or gets off.
In these breaks I dream the most beautiful dreams,
All, alas, abruptly interrupted.

Ah, sleep in an average, strange bed
In a third rate hotel!
One falls flat on the greasy divan, damp, slightly cock-eyed,
In the room there's a smell of prison,
The window's barred.
And it'd be stupid to open it because beggers can jump.

About midnight, pain wakes you,
It's in the ribs, made by the springs,
You feel your way and can't find the light.
Where are you? Which town is it?
You think you're still travelling and wait for the guard,
"What's the next station, please?"

Sometimes it's true, you're in the express!
In the sleeper. You decided to treat yourself.
At the window you recognise nothing,
The scenery may just as well

Be Italian, Swiss or even the moon.
Trees change from second to second,
Like guards of honour
At a hasty funeral,
Or like telegrams received in a battle
Where the result's uncertain.
You're the commander, you received them, opened them,
The subalterns are watching your mouth waiting for orders,
But the telegrams are ciphered
And you've forgotten the cipher of the leaves.

I only feel well when
Half-asleep, uncomfortable,
Standing on one foot on a blister
Strap-hanging, hung on a window-sill,
On a servant's stair,
Having to rush urgently God knows where,
Carrying four big suitcases full of useless things,
Relinquishing, because of them, the only thing
Of any importance: the umbrella . (It always rains cats and dogs,
                                        when you're a traveller.)

I only feel well when unwell,
Limping,
Bags under the eyes,
Thrown in the street by my own anxiety . . .

Always pushed about on roads like a kick up the arse,
Eyes bulging, as if I'd seen a miracle.

SYNCHRONIZATION

Everything about us is perfect
On this century's
Cinema screen:
Both in sound and image.

It's just that many times
With appearance on cue,
We start to act and talk sense –
But nothing's heard.
Your words on the screen run ahead
Or get stopped at customs.
At other times you find yourself speaking
Someone else's lines,
Which don't fit your mouth,
They're too big or too small.

Then far worse
Is when your voice begins to be heard
After you've emerged
From the projector's beam
Of sun.

It doesn't matter.
There are a few small defects
Of synchronization.
Perhaps in time we'll be able
To say exactly what we think,
And to speak
Even in our lifetime.

WE TALK ABOUT THE WEATHER

We've finished all topics of conversation,
Now let's talk about the weather,
Any of us can say something
About weather.

I, to start talking,
Will be of the opinion it'll rain,
Because I dreamt of a big cloud
Circling round my brow
Which always rained on me,
Soaking thoughts to the skin.

Someone
To contradict me, insists upon good weather.
For in the following three centuries,
The sky will be so bright
That we'll all see each other,
Without needing fireworks
To do so.

Someone talks to us about a dead leaf,
Which flies before the bare trees
And which none of us can keep –
Tomorrow it'll pass our street,
Let's go on the balcony
And watch it too.

And so we're able to hold a conversation,
We'll contradict each other and speak very loudly,
So that crickets inside us run away hurriedly.

The main thing is that silence never comes between us,
The main thing is to be happy.

THE INVISIBLE ONES

The royal throne is right there in my head,
Or to be more exact, it is my head,
It's all that's left
Of an area as vast as the eye can see.

And over it
How many invasions have spread,
How many trenches must I dig daily
To fill them all with sweat from my brow
– it's fresher, running, and much safer –
To raise turret walls round it,
And in the end defend it sword in hand.

Of course I fight the battle
With the barbarians.
As many as there are grains of sand,
Their numbers darken even the sun,
It's just that they can't be seen,
They're barbarians totally invisible,

That's why the battle's even more terrible
And even more a struggle for life and death,
It's just that I've no blood left to spill
Unless perhaps it's mine again
If I suddenly feel like suicide.

My one wish is that these efforts of mine
Be recorded in the struggle for independence,
And that important historical events
Be given their true significance.

ATAVISM

Looking out of the window has become a nervous tic,
Everyone's looking out of the window.
They read, they wash, they love, die
And from time to time they rush
To look out of the window.

What do you want to see?
Who are you staring at?
Stop thinking about it, who's coming's come,
Who had to go's gone,
What was to pass by, has passed by.
Leave the curtains,
Pull the blinds
And take your blood pressure once again.

Having seen everything, – rain, wars,
Sun, moles, events,
Always repeated exactly the same,
I can't believe mankind seriously wants
To see something else.
However there it is stuck to the window
With hollow eyes.

COMPETITION

One, two, three . . .
The hibernation competition has begun.
Everyone lock yourselves in your lair
And let's see who can hibernate the longest.

You know the competition rules:
No moving,
No dreaming,
No thinking.
Anyone caught thinking
Is out of the game and no longer our concern.

Like a pipe, you can only use
Your paw for sucking
To stimulate you in the deep understanding
Of this event.

I'm lucky to find myself near a bear,
Because when I've had enough of my paw,
I'll give it to him,
And use his,
Which as it happens is within the accepted norm
Of paws.
And although the Pharoah Cheops
Has the advantage of a few milleniums,
I also hope to overtake him
By an outstanding sprint,
Our famous sprint
In the field of hibernation.

*   *   *

Every year
Life salutes us
With 365 shots
Of sun.

It's a great event
Our arrival into the
Inanimate world,
And matter
Gives us our due
Honours.

The trees put on little flags
Of seasons,
In the air, rise oxygen bubbles
And coloured stars.

From the sea cheers are heard,
Waves carry banners.
Everything
Clamours to see us,
What more can I say?
It's a beautiful feast and unrivalled.

And we, moved,
For as long as the light lasts,
Stay standing
As for the national anthem.

TRUTH COMES TO LIGHT

Truth comes to light
Extremely slowly.
Following the movement technique of decomposure and rotting
Oil rises to the surface
But only after it's drowned.

* * *

When I want to have a rest
I'm ill.
I take to my bed.
Imagine how ill
I'll be
Dead!

WITH JUST ONE LIFE

Hold with both hands
The tray of each day
And pass in a line
In front of this counter.

There's enough sun
For everyone,
There's enough sky,
There's enough moon.

From the earth comes fragrance
Of luck, happiness, glory
Which tickles your nostrils
Temptingly.

So don't be miserly,
Live as your heart's stirred,
The prices are absurd.

For instance, with just one life
You can get
The most beautiful woman,
And a loaf.

SENTENCE

Each traveller in the tram
Looks identical to the one who sat there before him
On that very seat.

Either the speed's far too great,
Or the world's far too small.

Each has a threadbare neck caused
By the newspaper read behind him.
I'm aware of a newspaper in the neck
Turning and cutting my veins
With its edges.

THE RECKONING

There comes a time
When we have to draw a line under us
A black line
To do the summing up.

The few moments when you were about to be happy,
The few moments when we were nearly beautiful,
The few moments when we were almost a genius.
Occasionally we've met
Mountains, trees, water
(What ever happened to them? Do they still exist?)
Each adds up to a brilliant future –
Which we've lived.

A woman we've loved,
Plus the same woman who didn't love us
Equals zero.

A quarter of a year of studies
Makes several million fodder words
Whose widsom we've gradually eliminated.
And finally, a fate
Plus another fate (Now where does that come from?)
Equals two (Write one, carry one,
Perhaps, who knows, there is a life hereafter).

THE OLD ONES IN THE SHADE

You tire quickly, you forget easily,
You begin to talk alone,
You move your lips . . .
In the mirror you surprise yourself moving your lips.

I know roughly what it's going to be like when I'm old.
Every summer I experience one or two days a week
Of old age.
Wrinkled, dried out like a peach stone in the core
Of a juicy day.

A Ulysses with a mind like a sieve,
Forgetting where he was supposed to return,
Why he wanders on the sea
And whether it's before or after the Trojan wars.
A Ulysses with few chances of kissing the smoke leaving chimneys
Of his homelands.

You hesitate between adjusting your tie
And strangling yourself with it.

40 degrees in the sun! I come into the house
And with a last mental effort remember
What I'm called.
The sultry heat resembles old age.
The same sensations.

The carpet slips from under your feet
You trip over your slippers —
A nail is turning purple,
You seem to have a wobbling tooth.

There's a feeling of unity in summer,
We're all older,
Even the foetus in the womb of the mother.

THE ACTORS

How easy-going – the actors!
With their sleeves rolled up
How cleverly they're able to be us!

I've never seen a more perfect kiss
Than by actors in the third act,
When emotions are beginning
To clear.

Stained with oil
In authentic caps,
Carrying out all kinds of jobs,
They enter and exit on lines
Which roll from their feet like rugs.

So natural is their death on stage
That, compared to this perfection,
The ones in graveyards
Seem to move,
Those who wear forever the make-up of tragedy,
The real dead!

We're stiff and awkward in just one life!
We don't know how to live it properly anyway.
We talk a load of nonsense or keep silent years on end.
And embarrassed and unattractive
We don't know what the hell to do with our hands.

PRAYER

Saints,
Let me join your ranks
At least as an extra.

You're getting old,
Perhaps you feel the pain of age
Painted on your bodies
In so many stages.

Let me carry out
The humblest jobs
In nooks and crannies.

I could for instance,
Eat the light
At the Last Supper,
And blow out your haloes
When the service is over.

And, from time to time,
At half a wall's distance,
Cup my hands to my mouth
And holler, once for the believers
And once for the unbelievers:
Hallelujah! Hallelujah!

SHAKESPEARE

Shakespeare created the world in seven days.

On the first day he made the sky, the mountains and the depths
                                             of the soul.
On the second day he made rivers, seas, oceans
And the other emotions –
And gave them to Hamlet, Julius Caesar, Anthony, Cleopatra
                                             and Ophelia,
To Othello and others,
To be master over them, with their descendants,
For ever and ever.
On the third day he gathered all the people
And taught them to savour:
The taste of happiness, love, despair,
The taste of jealousy, fame and so on,
Until all tasting was finished.
Then some late-comers arrived.
The creator patted their heads with compassion,
Saying the only roles left for them were the
Literary critics
Who could then demolish his work.
The fourth and fifth day he reserved for laughter.
He allowed clowns
To tumble,
He allowed kings, emperors
And other unfortunates to amuse themselves.
On the sixth day he completed the administration:
He set up a tempest,
He taught King Lear
How to wear a straw crown.
As there were a few leftovers from the creation of the world
He designed Richard III.
On the seventh day he took stock to see what else might be done.
The theatre directors had already covered the earth with posters,
And Shakespeare thought that after so much effort
He deserved to see a performance.
But first, as he was overtired,
He decided to die a little.

THE RUNNER

A deserted field,
Trodden down like a road,
And here and there
A book,

At great distances,
A basic book,
Firm as rock.

One is coming, panting with muscles,
Healthy as a new god,
And spits on it,
On each one in a row,
Steps on them heavenly.

He tires, he's had enough,
The field stretches ahead, deserted,
Trodden down like a road.
The runner collapses, dies,
Becomes a basic book, the last word,
A sign over which one cannot pass anymore.

Panting is heard,
From beyond a figure appears,
A runner stops, spits on the sign
And disappears over the horizon.

FRIENDS

Let's commit suicide, I said to my friends,
Today we've really understood each other,
We've been very depressed,
Never again will we reach
Such a peak of perfection
And it's a pity to waste the opportunity.

I think the bathroom's the most tragic place,
Let's do it like the enlightened Romans
Who opened their veins
While discussing the essence of love.
Look, I've warmed the water,
Let's make a start, dear friends, I'll count to three.

In hell I was somewhat surprised to find myself alone.
Perhaps some people don't die quite so easily
I told myself, or have ties.
I couldn't have made a mistake: making a pact's got to mean
                                                    something.
But time went on. . .

I can assure you, it was quite hard for me in hell,
Especially at the start, as I was on my own,
There was no one there I could talk to,
But gradually I was accepted, made friends.

A very tightly knit group,
We discussed all sorts of theoretical questions,
We felt great,
We even got around to suicide.

And again, I found myself alone, in purgatory
Looking for a few kindred spirits,
Although the purgatorians were quite suspicious –
With their uncertain situation
Between two worlds –
A girl loves me, she's very beautiful.
We share moments of great ecstasy – unbelievable, fantastic!

And I feel almost like saying to her. . .
But having seen it all before, I let her do it first,
I wait and commit suicide afterwards,
Yet the girl somehow manages to come back to life —
And then I'm on my own in heaven —
No one's ever reached that far before,
I'm the first, the world exists only as a project,
Something very, very vague
In God's head,
I'm getting very friendly with him lately.

There's sadness at all levels,
Even God's desperate,
I look into his empty eyes and there lose myself.
He slips roaring down the precipice of my deaths,
We understand each other perfectly,
God, I think we've reached perfection,
You first,
How about leaving it all in the dark?

THE ILLNESS

I can feel something dying, Doctor,
It's here just around my being,
All my inside hurts,
During the day it's the sun that hurts,
And in the night it's the moon and stars.

I get a sharp pain in the cloud on the sky
Which I didn't even notice until today,
And I wake up every morning
With a sort of winter feeling.

I've taken all kinds of medicine, but it's done no good,
I've hated, and loved, I learned to read,
And I even read some books,
I talked to people and had a think,
I was good and I was handsome. . .

But none of it did any good, doctor,
And I've spent no end of years on it,

I think I must have caught death
One day
When I was born.

CHESS

I move a white day,
He moves a black day.
I advance with a dream,
He takes it to war.
He attacks my lungs,
I think for about a year in hospital.
I make a brilliant combination
And win a black day.
He moves a disaster
And threatens me with cancer
(Which moves for the moment in the shape of a cross)
But I put a book before him
He's obliged to retreat.
I win a few more pieces,
But, look, half my life
Is taken.
– If I give you check, you lose your optimism,
He tells me.
– It doesn't matter, I joke,
I'll do the castling of feelings.
Behind me my wife, children,
The sun, the moon and other onlookers
Tremble for every move I make.

I light a cigarette
And continue the game.

SYMMETRY

I was walking
When suddenly two roads opened
In front of me:
One to the right,
And one to the left,
Conforming to all rules of symmetry.

I stopped,
Screwed up my eyes,
Pursed my lips,
Coughed,
And set off on the one to the right
(Just the one I shouldn't have taken
As was later proved.)

I went on as best I could,
No need to give details.
And then in front of me opened two
Precipices:
One to the right,
One to the left.
I threw myself into the left,
Without even blinking, or jumping,
Just like a big heap into the one on the left,
Which, unfortunately, wasn't lined with feathers!
Crawling, I set off again.
I crawled for some time,
And suddenly in front of me
Two wide roads opened.
"I'll show you!" – I told myself,
And with grim determination,
I set off again on the one to the left.
Wrong, very wrong, the one on my right
Was the proper one, the real road, the great road.
And at the first crossroads
I gave myself totally
To the one on the right. Then the same again,
The other should have been the one, the other. . .

Now the food's almost gone,
My walking stick's aged,
Its buds no longer appear,
So I can rest in their shade.
When I become desperate.
Stones wear out my bones,
They creak and grumble at me
For one mistake after another. . .

And look, in front of me, opening again
Two skies:
One to the right,
One to the left.

*   *   *

I'm sorry for the butterflies
When I switch the light off,
And for the bats
When I switch it on. . .
Can't I move an inch
Without offending anyone?

So many strange things happen,
That I could always stay
Head in hands,
But an anchor thrown from heaven
Pulls them down. . .

The time isn't yet ripe
To rip the canvases,
Leave it.

Nichita Stănescu
(b. 1933 d. 1983)

A KIND OF QUIET IN BYBLOS

The diplomatic commuting has ended.
The whirlwind of burned smoke behind the plane
descends and speeds stunning
the dust on the sands.
Mothers in black, lie in wait at airports
watching through the curtain of rays.
The mutual exchange
of bodies of murdered soldiers
has begun.
Sacred scarabs roll again
in the desert,
earthly globes
the size of an adolescent's eye.
Millions of sacred scarabs, in the desert
roll millions of earthly globes
the size of an adolescent's eye.
Mothers in black lie in wait
at airports.
The mutual exchange of bodies
of murdered soldiers
has begun.
On beaches, on rocks, on sands,
are tanning the sacramental bodies
of adolescents,
their mothers, still dressed in white,
in red, in green and in violet,
lie in wait from a distance, sacramental and
with a hand to the mouth,
The dust from the sand shimmers
with red, iridescent gold.

SAD LOVE

Let's leave objectivity to the cog wheel,
to the bolt and the seal.
If time slips by the way it slips by me,
you don't have the right to watch me.

Let's leave to the happy ones the right
to drink water
because only they have mouths
and only they are thirsty.

But when I sleep, when I sleep
so deep
when I sleep the way I sleep
you surely don't have the right to get up
and leave.

THE LIGHTNING AND THE COLD

Dedicated to Nicolae Manolescu, literary critic

All of us in the courtyard, suddenly
uneasy, felt the presence of the wing.
It happened one Monday afternoon
a year ago.
For such a long time, especially in the evenings,
without saying a word to each other,
especially in the evenings, evening after evening,
we felt the uneasy presence of the wing
among ourselves in the courtyard.
Discretely we searched in the maple tree, in the barn, through the
                                            sky-light,
or even under the big armchair in the dining room.
Also, we searched behind the family picture
in the rich frame, among the women's dresses in the wardrobe,
behind the velvet curtain, colured deep cherry.
Seemingly looking everywhere but there,
while talking about anything but that,
the presence of the wing was and still is unnerving us.
That's why the radio is always turned up,
and the noisy pump in the yard left to run.
Cats and dogs increased because of this,
and the bulb at the entrance
at night's left on.
Only recently, after a whole year,
while hurriedly leaving, called out by a patient,
I suddenly felt at my back
its cold breeze.
I stopped at the corner of the street
and turned my face like lightning to the house.
Ah, you, cold and lightning.
The angel is the very wall of the house,
the large wall, cut in the middle by a square window.
It's this very wall,
this one with the square window!
It's the very one
watching me, coldly.

AH, HOW MUCH WATER

Time becomes time
when it transforms into grass, into water,
into trees and into stones.
It is the only thing which has movement within it,
it is the only thing which passes
which ties and unties us
which becomes pregnant
by all that it meets on the way,
inventing its way,
giving birth to its way.
The only tangible thing is time,
objects are its movement.
Tigris and Euphrates,
ah, how much water!

FROM AN EVENING

I had to calm the dogs which had become restless
for no reason at all.
I had to ask for my glass to be changed
because suddenly I got a shock from it.
I had to look twice
to see if indeed it had passed by, very close to me,
near the lamplight from the garden,
that bird which proved that it had passed
and wasn't fluorescent green, as it had seemed to me,
but its usual grey.
That's why I'm writing this letter to you now
To ask you not to think about me anymore in the evenings
with such thoughts
and to assure you once more
that I haven't killed he whom I promised you
I'd leave alive.

Good bye.

SELF-PORTRAIT

I am nothing more than
a stain of blood
that speaks.

A CONFESSION

I can't yet raise an anthem to the stillness
for which I long and for which I hunger.
Not one house where I've stayed
kept me long inside it.
I long to be able to live
in my own words,
but clumsily through their doors
my body leans towards the animal kingdom.
Gladly I'd render to dogs that which is dogs
and to the maple trees that which is theirs,
but for me the howling of dogs is banned,
and the smell of maple trees forbidden.
I'd have to be able to rise much higher,
I'd have to throw away this ballast, –
but just the thought that what's above
might be exactly like that below, –
troubles me, so that I find
every throw has no direction
and static is every rejection.

UNTAMING

From too much black I'm white
from too much sun I'm night
from too much life more dead am I
only in dream myself am I
come to me from head to heel
to roll ourselves into a wheel
come to me, you, yet without you
so that I can be me, with me
O leaven, leaven, leaven
on my inferno be a heaven
O, stay, stay, stay
my palms nail and lay
on the cross of flesh
while the world rests.

SONG

The thinking body, now ugly, had evolved,
the words were said in an ancient and barbaric tongue.
To live had become 'I had lived' –
Inside me death had begun.

A patch of shadow crossed over me;
it was only from a vulture rising to fly
which was interrupting, gracefully,
the place where I was born,
from that where I shall die.

Sun, burning with cries, who keens for you
with his eyes?

SHE

Just now, just now
when I love her most,
just now I lied to her.
Just now, just now
when she's most fond of me,
just now I cast a shadow on her.
Just now, just now
when she's thinking about me
I'm singing my sorrows.
Just now, just now
when she's the most beautiful in the world
of my stars,
I go blind.
Just now, just now
when I feel her grace
penetrating all the walls of the town
I go deaf.
Just now, just now
when I feel that she is longing for me
I'm hurting my friends
unable to bear how much I long for her.
Just now, just now
when for my sake she irons
the gingham dress,
I stand and clean spears with petrol
To throw them at vultures and beasts.
Just now, just now
when I should be
filled with tender running,
I'm reaching for dreams
for fear of being happy.
Just now, just now
when she radiates light from her heart,
I read about the nova
and all the exploded stars
and I stretch like the longest street in town
and I pave
and dress in snow and ice,
especially ice,

especially ice, especially ice,
so that she, darling and divine
in passing, slips,
falls and hurts her ankle,
which, God,
I haven't kissed for such a long time.
After all,
who has the courage to kiss an ankle
if it isn't limping?!

WATCHING HER – MY MOTHER

On this loved one fell
all the time I have lived,
on this loved one shone
all my lived time.
I couldn't tear my glance away
from this loved one
I had eyes only to see her
my loved one.
I had arms only to embrace her
my loved one.
Suddenly, I saw my mother see her
this loved one.
On this loved one
time falls and snows.
Looking at my loved one
my mother cries.

MISTAKEN SKY

The vultures were flying upturned
and with claws turned upwards
to steal, as they would lambs,
the star with undulated light;

To steal, from above, as they would lambs,
the light of my eyes.

The vultures were flying upturned
and on their backs through the sky
their spines dropped
and rubbed against my breastbone.

Their sky was my body of flesh,
their earth the light of my eyes
from above.

HIEROGLYPHIC

What loneliness
not to understand the meaning
when there is a meaning

And what loneliness
to be blind in broad daylight, –
and deaf, what loneliness
when the song's in full swing

But not to understand
when there's nothing to understand
and to be blind in the middle of the night
and deaf when silence is absolute, –
Oh, loneliness of loneliness!

Ion Stoica
(b. 1936)

THE SPELL

Who e'er may do you harm
Let hemlock spring from his bed,
May the good stop his turn,
And night lie long in his head,
May all his days be mad
And draw luck that's bad
Like a hare draws cabbages to him,
May a stork's nest in winter hold him,
Let fire burn him!
And for you, good maiden,
Dreams of the moon with sleep are laden,
Above fields of tranquillity,
Autumns with a taste of honey
May dress you now in peaceful swathes,
May you have the stars for guards
Near your slumbers with the flowers
Awaiting you in the early hours
Herald of happy days above
The narrow beam of sun,
With news of love
From me will come

THE TRIAL

Do you confess that from time to time
You step out of line,
And profess
That the sighs of the world bore you?
— I confess!
— Do you deny that you set yourself high
Above others and on
Request would dare for the whole world
Acclaimed by it?
— I don't deny it!
— Do you admit that sometimes you dream night
After night, conquering yourself in flight
Believing
That in the gardens of heaven you can sit?
— This I admit!
— Do you recall in how many meadows
You forgot the commandments,
Stealing
Secret loves
Like an outlaw, too!
— I do!
— Does it happen in your forest you stand looking
In vain for oaks fearless of lopping
And winds of disgust burn under your brow?
— It does now.
— Don't you ever creep under the evenings
Full of mud and sighing under burdens,
Wondering
If your star was heavenless?
— Oh, yes!
— Isn't it true that in your humble mind
One day you found a knife
And still considering yourself pure and kind
You kept mute?
— It's the truth!
— Sometimes during long nights you search
But yourself you cannot reach
And you're afraid
And in your room the silence screams?

— That's how it seems.

*

The verdict is unanimous:
The greatest punishment applying:
An eternity of waiting
In an eternity of loneliness

I SHOULD HAVE LIKED. . .

I should have liked to cut the light
To make me a hood from that night
When the seeds of the world burst open
And began their eternal flight,
And to have been at midhour,
In its first innocence,
When under the eyes of day
Not one moment had begun
And to burn in four winds
By horizons of waiting,
Guilty of the beginning
Of each drop of sun,
And to have cried a sea,
To have bled in rivers,
And to have melted through time
In bewildered flowing,
To have felt pain
Petrifying into mountains
And the spring of dreams
In the garden of the first wedding,
And near the condemned shadow
To have changed the night
Heavy with hatred
Into a flowering leaf
And from mists of legend
In the flow of history
To see myself clearly in the water of the day
As in my mirror whose duty's
Not to wound me any more with
Cold light, waxen faces,
My moments able to look down,
My sky to have had a ladder

DECALOGUE

Thou shalt not take anything but dreams on thy way,
Put as many as you like in your treasure hold,
If the road is long and hard
They keep you from hunger, thirst and cold.
Thou shalt give only words as gifts
Their river does not freeze,
Among all your wealth,
For time's reckoning keep only these.
Thou shalt not stay in a lone star,
The highest is still falling,
Worlds are cut out from the lights
And from unfulfilled waiting.
Thou shalt not come from a forgotten night,
Go, together with the day through the copse,
It is a soul of the day where
All the moments of the world are pressed.
Thou shalt not listen to the voice of cold winters,
Fear of time slipping on the snow,
When the sand from the hours is burning you
Stay in the orchard under autumn's apple bough.
Thou shalt not fly all the summer in the flock,
Alone one evening cut across the field,
Without the terrors of night and wind
Joy has no price to yield.
Thou shalt not forget to look in mirrors,
In eyes, the book and the well,
From your face out of the depths, unknown
Thou shalt not run in the world afar;
Thou shalt not say that importance uplifts you
Deifying you in your noons,
Only the clouds make the peak forget
How near it is to the valley.
Thou shalt not swear on anything ever,
The gods are dying, lowered in the word.
The witness to all is only the distance
And cannot be reached by face and by wind;
Thou shalt not die before death
Keep the law which comes from the sky,
While the white light's within you
Thou shalt not die, not die, not die.

97

TRAPEZE

It's as if one's always
In a circus ring,
In a round valley walled by people,
On high, the trapeze,
In a noon of eyes,
Flying above hills of men,
Over walls alive with hope,
Holding their breath;
In your ears resound
The canons of the hearts beneath,
Because silence has leaden blood,
One aches with the uneasiness
Of those who call you to descend
And nothing seems easier
Than to give yourself to the void below

ORBIT

On the hour's threshold
Cry moments of yesterday
Lost from the fold,
Under the noise of the day
Valleys of silence
Vanish away;
On the threshold of love
A bitter tear
Is searching for home,
In a narrow gleam
The destiny of a star
Is stone;
A flight of words
Is heard passing
Through the sky much closer,
A face following
With eyes of air
And water;
Envious light
Is heard coming
From eternal watching,
In me is the night
When ways I wander
With pain;
Total unease in me
With a voice of steel
Calls me to be bridegroom
And all things are possible
And all things forbidden
Ad infinitum;
Towards seas of temptation
Which always soothe
The sad stream's glance,
I am held in orbit
By a heavy ball
Of chance.